HANDWRITING ANALYSIS

by Dorothy Sara

Manufactured in the United States of America

ISBN 0-89009-496-9

Arrangement has been made to publish this edition by Castle Books, a division of Book Sales Inc. of Secaucus, New Jersey

SEPTEMBER – 1983

Contents

Introduction

Seeking a simple definition of *handwriting analysis* I looked under the word *graphology* in the dictionary on my desk, and it reads: "The study of handwriting for the purpose of character analysis." Then I went to the reference room of the public library where they have huge, scholarly volumes of dictionaries, and the definition I found there reads: "The science of estimating character by studying the handwriting."

Actually we might call it *mind writing* instead of *handwriting,* as it is the brain which impels the hand to write. The brain transmits impulses to the arm and hand, and every movement of writing is controlled by the motor nervous system.

The handwriting expresses the personality just as it may be expressed in the way a person talks, laughs, walks, and makes other outward gestures which betray the inner personality. Benjamin Disraeli wrote, "Handwriting bears an analogy to the character of the writer, as all voluntary actions are characteristic."

Graphology may be said to be both a science and an art; it is a scientific method of analyzing the formations in a handwriting, but its interpretation is an art. Each formation in the writing has its individual meaning, yet the analysis cannot be based only on separate individual signs in the handwriting; they must be interpreted in relative proportion one to the other, to sum up the totality of the personality. A certain "t" bar may reflect one trait in one specimen of handwriting, but it may not signify the same meaning in another writing when that "t" bar is correlated to hundreds of other signs in the handwriting.

While the original term *graphology* expresses *handwriting analysis*, in recent years other words have been coined, such as *graphodiagnosis*, *psychographology*, and *graphoanalysis*. Though graphologists use these other names for advertising their work, their methods are based on the original graphological concepts, as far as making an analysis of handwriting is concerned. Sometimes a handwriting analyst is called a *handwriting expert;* but the work of the latter is in a different category. The handwriting expert examines documents for purposes of forgery and other legal matters; but the expert may not be able to analyze a handwriting for its personality traits. Some handwriting analysts are also experts, some handwriting experts are also analysts; but the two terms are not necessarily inclusive.

Graphology is a subsidiary in the field of psychology. Some graphologists may have training in psychology and in the use of other projective personality tests (such as Rorschach, Thematic Apperception Test, etc.). While these are fine adjuncts to have, they are not necessary for the graphologist whose work lies in the analysis of the handwriting itself. Some psychologists, psychiatrists, personnel directors, marriage counselors, and vocational aptitude testers are trained graphologists and use handwriting analysis in connection with their work; but those who are not so trained often make use of the services of a handwriting analyst, in the same way as a physician calls on the skills of a bacteriologist and other laboratory workers in aiding him to come to a fuller diagnosis.

While any high school child can learn what a certain "i" dot means or what a large capital letter means, simply by reading this book, it does not qualify that young person to make an analysis of the totality of the personality. This applies as well to adults who do not have psychological training. Yet, an adult who spends a lot of time in other fields where there is contact with people of all ages and all sorts, and then studies handwriting analysis, may utilize the experience gained in "living and working" even though there is no formal training in psychology. Often the one who is "educated by experience" may do a much keener job of analyzing a handwriting than the person who has only "book learning."

The important factor is that the graphologist must be entirely objective, must not have a single-tracked approach to handwriting analysis but must be sufficiently versed in knowing people to make the graphological analysis a true picture of the inner personality.

Handwriting analysis is not as new a subject as is usually implied; it is new in the English-speaking countries, but there is a long background of literature in European countries which deals with handwriting analysis. There are not many places where the subject can be studied, though this situation (I am optimistic) may be overcome as the general public is made aware of the function of a handwriting analyst and the good use to which an analysis may be put in helping people understand their inner selves.

There are not enough schools where this subject can be studied, so it is through private lessons or correspondence lessons that one must learn how to analyze handwriting.

However, there is currently one American institution of learning where graphology is taught as part of its Psychology Department; that is at the New School For Social Research in the city of New York. Also there is study going on in Switzerland, in the University of Zurich, where in 1963 a London industrialist, Siegmund G. Warburg, endowed the European Foundation of Graphological Science and Application in order to further the development of graphology. Mr. Warburg experienced much aid from graphologists in their analyses of people with whom he was dealing in business, which impelled him to endow this foundation so others could reap the same benefits.

When I became interested in handwriting analysis, through a chance remark made by a friend over thirty years ago, there was no school to turn to, so I went to my favorite source—the public library—and found a book on the shelf which was written by DeWitt B. Lucas, titled *Handwriting and Character*. I studied and studied this book, fascinated by the subject, but felt isolated in not knowing where to go for further knowledge. One day the newspaper listed a lecture on handwriting analysis to be given by Louise Rice at a business girls' club. I attended that meeting, which was a turning point of my life. I met Louise Rice (one of the hardy pioneers of graphology in this country); she invited me to join a group of fledgling graphologists who studied and worked with her. She is now gone, but her influence lingers on, and this book is dedicated to Louise Rice.

Dorothy Sara
NEW YORK, 1967

CHAPTER ONE

Background of Handwriting Analysis

Handwriting analysis is usually considered to be a contemporary science. But it has a long history. The one who is research-minded will discover references to the subject dating back many centuries, in the philosophical writings of occidental and oriental scholars.

Aristotle, the Greek philosopher, in the third century B.C. wrote, "Spoken words are symbols of mental experience; written words, the symbols of spoken words. Just as all men do not have the same speech sounds, neither do they all have the same writing."

In 120 A.D., C. Suetonius Tranquillus, the historian of the first twelve Caesars, in examining the handwriting of the Emperor Octavius Augustus, said, "He does not separate the words, nor carry over to the next line any excess letters. Instead he places them under the final word and he ties them to it with a stroke."

In the eleventh century we find the words of the Chinese philosopher and painter, Kuo Jo-hsu, "Handwriting infallibility can show whether it comes from a person who is noble-minded or one who is vulgar."

At the beginning of the seventeenth century in Italy the first recorded systematic detailing of handwriting analysis appeared, in a study titled *Ideographia* which was written by Alderisius Prosper and published in Bologna. In 1622 Camillo Baldi, a physician and professor at the University of Bologna, wrote a small treatise with a long title, *How to know the nature and qualities of a person by looking at a letter which he has written.*

Neither of these works met with widespread recognition, though some wandering magicians did make use of them by giving handwriting interpretation consultations on character as they would go from castle to castle to perform and entertain.

But the work of these Italian scholars did not go into complete oblivion. We find writings in the eighteenth century by Lavater in his *Physiognomic Fragments,* and by Grohmann (a churchman in Wittenberg) in his treatise titled *Examination of the Possibility of Inferring Character from Handwriting.*

People in various fields started to show an interest in the relationship between handwriting and character traits. The painter, Thomas Gainsborough, liked to keep on his easel a letter written by the subject of his portrait.

In 1820 Goethe said in one of his letters, "There can be no doubt that the handwriting of a person has some relation to his mind and character; that from it one may conceive at least some idea of his manner of being and acting, just as one must recognize not alone appearance and features, but also bearing, voice, even bodily movement as being significant and congruent with the total individuality."

Sir Walter Scott in 1827 wrote in his novel, *Chronicles of Canongate,* "I could not help thinking . . . that something of a man's character may be conjectured from his handwriting. That neat but crowded and constrained small-hand argued a man of good conscience, well-regulated passions, and, to use his own phrase, an upright walk in life; but it also indicated narrowness of spirit, inveterate prejudice, and hinted at some degree of intolerance, which, though not natural to the disposition, had arisen out of a limited education."

We find authors and poets referring to analysis of handwriting in their writings, among them Stefan Zweig, Edgar Allan Poe, George Sand, Thomas Mann, Lion Feuchtwanger, Alexander Dumas, Emile Zola, and many others. They may have arrived at their conclusions through intuitive response to the formations of the handwriting, rather than through knowledge of systematic analysis; but the results they achieved were indicative of their intelligent interest in the field of interpretation of character traits.

EUROPEAN PIONEERS OF GRAPHOLOGY

About the middle of the nineteenth century a group of French churchmen came together to study handwriting in an effort to find the relationship between character traits and their graphic expression. This group was composed of Cardinal Regnier, Archbishop of Cambrai, Bishop Soudinet of Amiens, and the Abbé Flandrin.

Their investigations led to successful interpretations and they received much recognition throughout France. The Abbé Jean-Hippolyte Michon of Paris, a disciple of the Abbé Flandrin, continued the work started by this group. Michon collected thousands of specimens of handwriting over a period of about thirty years; he then formulated a system of analyzing the different strokes in the handwriting and published his findings in two books in 1872 and 1878, which created a stir at the time among people who became interested in this way of relating human elements of character to formations of handwriting.

The Abbé Michon coined the word *graphology* to designate *handwriting analysis,* and among contemporary graphologists he is looked upon as the father of modern graphology.

Michon had many avid disciples, some of whom formed the *Société Graphologique,* which functioned until the Second World War.

One of Michon's followers, Jules Crépieux-Jamin, felt that Michon's findings were too closely confined to the individual signs in the handwriting, such as a certain "t" bar crossing, or an "i" dot, were too fixed in scope, and did not always mean the same in each handwriting (when correlated to the other signs). Crépieux-Jamin elaborated on the work of Michon so that emphasis was placed not only on the individual letter formation but on the overall aspect of the handwriting as well. He said of Michon's work, "The study of the elements (of handwriting) is to graphology what the study of the alphabet is to reading of prose." He also recognized that handwriting analysis revealed the psychological and not the physiological personality of the writer. This fact led to the knowledge that a handwriting does not reveal the sex or the chronological age of the writer.

Another important contribution made by Crépieux-Jamin was his success in persuading Alfred Binet (founder of intelligence tests) to investigate graphology, to test the assumption that there is a correlation between specific handwriting signs and specific character traits. Binet's conclusions were in the affirmative, which brought much favor and respect to the subject of graphology, and it was now regarded by some scholars as "the science of the future."

The French graphologists held almost exclusive sway until almost the end of the nineteenth century, at which time an interest arose in Germany, especially with the works of three men: Wilhelm Preyer, a child psychologist and a professor of physiology at Jena; Georg Meyer, a psychiatrist; and Ludwig Klages, a philosopher. They approached the subject of graphology from a psychological viewpoint, from the "total individuality" concept rather than merely delineating a character from the strokes themselves.

These men did extensive research, they wrote papers and books which were acclaimed in psychological circles; while they based their work on the pioneer studies of the French graphologists, they did not give full credit to them and in some of their writings even failed to mention the names of their French graphological predecessors, who did the initial work in this new scientific field.

It is to Wilhelm Preyer that we owe the concept of "brain writing" as he conducted experiments with people who had physical handicaps, such as no arms or legs, and he had them write with the pen held in the mouth or the toes; the results thus gained show the same signs in the handwriting as would have been apparent had the person been able to hold the pen in his hand and do the writing.

In 1896 the *Deutsche Graphologische Gesellschaft* was formed, and to promote interest in the theory and practice of handwriting analysis they issued *Graphologische Monatshefte* for their membership.

The German graphologists' books have not been translated into English; yet they have been widely read in Europe as well as in this country.

Coming to the twentieth century we find intensive study in the field of graphology going on in Germany and France, also in Switzerland where Dr. Max Pulver, a professor at the University of Zurich, contributed greatly to the study and teaching of graphology. Dr. Pulver's books are written in German, and are not translated into English.

We are indebted to some fine graphological books, written in English, by Robert Saudek and by Hans Jacoby, published in England and in this country.

In 1914 renewed interest was shown in Italy when a priest, Father Girolamo Moretti, published his *Treatise on Graphology*. He continued intensive research and made about 300,000 analyses of handwriting specimens during a period covering fifty years. The unique contribution made by Father Moretti to the literature of graphology occurred in 1952 when he wrote a book, *The Saints through Their Handwriting,* which showed his analyses of thirty-two saints. This book was subsequently translated into the English language and published in this country in 1964.

About 1920 an interest in graphology arose in Hungary; psychologists who knew of the work of other European graphologists started investigations on their own, and they would use handwriting analysis as a supplemental tool to the information which they got from their other psychological testing techniques. They founded an association of graphologists, who then started an institute in Budapest to do handwriting research. Among this group was Dr. Klara Roman, who later came to this country, and her book, *Handwriting—A Key to Personality,* was published here in English. Dr. Roman constructed a device called *graphodyne* which she used in the special study of handwriting development of school children.

GRAPHOLOGY IN AMERICA

Handwriting analysis was almost unknown in this country before the twentieth century, and its introduction to the United States had to be done in such a way that it could catch the attention of as many people as possible, to create an awareness of the subject, rather than relegate it to the "test tube" clinical methods of a laboratory where it could take too many years (as evidenced by the long time lapses when graphology was brought to the attention of the Europeans).

Popular books were written by various writers in the early days of struggle for graphology to become known here. Books were authored by pioneering Hugo von Hagen, Leslie French, Louise Rice, and Harrington Keane (who used the pseudonym of "Grapho"). Louise Rice conducted columns which were syndicated in newspapers throughout the country; readers would send in ten cents to get a short analysis (and I was one of a group of young graphologists who wrote these analyses). They were valid analyses, though rather short; but their purpose of interesting people in the science of graphology struck on fertile ground. It was not too long before clinical psychologists started to show an interest in the possibilities of graphology as a supplemental tool.

Books on the subject started coming in from Europe to the United States, in their native languages, and some from London where there was sufficient interest to have books on graphology printed in the English language. An early experimenter in this field was June Downey, at the University of Iowa, who published *Graphology and the Psychology of Handwriting* in 1919.

A similar investigation was done in 1930 and 1931 by Gordon Allport and Philip E. Vernon, at the Harvard Psychological Clinic. These two men collaborated with Robert Saudek and other professional graphologists. They showed courage in doing their experiments at a time when graphology was not held in highest esteem in this country.

Robert Saudek became the editor of the publication, *Character and Personality*, published at Duke University, which dealt with the serious and scientific aspects of psychological graphology.

By this time the United States had the benefit of graphologists who came from Europe. Among them was Klara Roman, mentioned heretofore, as well as Werner Wolff whose book, *Diagram of the Unconscious,* and Ulrich Sonnemann whose book, *Handwriting Analysis as a Psychodiagnostic Tool,* were both published in English.

Significant research is being done in ways of measuring rhythm, speed, and pressure of writing; thicknesses of strokes, etc.; and scales and other devices are being considered to further such clinical work. In 1942 "movement scales" were devised and tests made by Thea Stein-Lewinson and Joseph Zubin. Recently, for a period of about five years, Huntington Hartford supported a Handwriting Institute in New York (comprised of psychologists, graphologists, researchers) for the purpose of testing strokes, movements, and other details which the graphological researcher finds necessary for the further development of the science.

TODAY'S GRAPHOLOGICAL PICTURE

Research goes on, thanks to the American graphologists who are interested in clinical study and to the many European colleagues who are now here to give us the benefit of their many years' head-start on us. Some research goes on to find correlation between physical and mental ailments and handwriting indications; though this is in the clinical stage and not in use as yet for the general public, until conclusive evidences are absolute.

Graphology still needs to be "sold" to the public in addition to those who are in the field of psychological personality testing. It is sometimes necessary to use the practical (and perhaps blatant) manner of salesmanship to tell people how valuable handwriting analysis can be as a supplemental tool in the field of psychology.

Some graphologists are qualified to do research work. Others, like myself, are not so oriented, but we are equipped to do handwriting analyses by mail, assist psychologists and psychiatrists through analyses of the handwritings of their patients, give lectures to groups, write articles for popular magazines (thus reaching thousands of people of all areas who might otherwise never hear about graphology), and appear on television and radio broadcasts to let the listeners know of the availability of graphology.

It is just as necessary to do this kind of "selling to the public" as it is to continue research on the subject in the clinical laboratories.

Not too many years ago in this country the handwriting analyst was not given much of a welcome; today the graphologist is recognized as a needed worker in the field of personality testing. And this book is for the person who may never become a clinical or practicing handwriting analyst, but who will be made aware of the purpose of handwriting analysis.

CHAPTER TWO

What Handwriting Analysis Reveals

The basic traits of people are revealed in the formations of handwriting. The inner personality of a person is individual and different from other people, and the handwriting formations are distinctly different as the person's fingerprints are different.

Some people are shocked on receiving an analysis when it does not portray the outer personality of the writer but seems to give an entirely different picture. This may take place when a person has a superficial outer self, covering up the basic inner personality. Therefore, a handwriting analysis tells what the person is and not what others may think he or she is, or what sort of "playacting" that person may perform in trying to impress people with a glittering outer manner.

REASONS WHY ANALYSIS IS MADE

The reasons why people have their handwritings (or the handwritings of others) analyzed are as varied as are the individual facets of any person's life.

A man may meet a girl and want to know about her,

before he starts his courting. Or, in reverse, the girl may meet the boy, and wants to know about him.

Employers send the handwritings of job applicants, or of their employees, in order to better know how to place the right person in the right job. Usually the employer uses a battery of tests and includes graphology as a supplemental tool. The advantage of a handwriting analysis in such cases is that the applicant or employee does not have to be present when the analysis is made (as is the case with most other tests). Thus, the applicant is not tense, not embarrassed, and the handwriting analysis is a confidential matter between the employer and the graphologist.

College students write to ask if they are majoring in the right fields, and to find out if their desires for a certain career are suitable to their abilities and emotions.

People who want to change jobs write to a graphologist, in order to know if they will be able to handle the new job. And secretaries ask about their employers, usually not to be critical about them but in a desire to understand them and thus perform their own duties better.

Parents want to know about their children, and children want to know about their parents. Wives and husbands want to know about themselves and their mates. Usually this is prompted by a desire to have better relationships in family life.

USED IN PSYCHOLOGICAL TESTING, PERSONNEL SCREENING, FAMILY AND PERSONAL RELATIONSHIPS

Psychologists social workers, psychiatrists, marriage counselors also avail themselves of the services of graphologists (if they do not have a knowledge of the subject of handwriting analysis themselves). They find this enables them to have a quick start in understanding their patients or clients, before they begin their therapeutic aid to these people.

An interesting phase of the work of a graphologist has recently opened up because of the forced retirement plans when people reach a certain age. Many prospective retirees write and ask what new fields they may enter, as hobbies or perhaps part-time jobs.

Until about thirty-five years ago, the services of a handwriting analyst were confined almost exclusively to workers in the field of psychology who were willing to give this "new testing device" a try; also to American branches of European firms who had (in their own countries) used graphologists for personnel screening; or to people of higher education who were willing to investigate this way of finding out about themselves and their friends and families. But now, due to the efforts of handwriting analysts to popularize the subject, there are no longer any lines drawn between those who avail themselves of graphology and those who hesitate to use it. Handwriting analyses are universally requested by people of all ages, in all walks of life, in all geographical areas, and for every imaginable sort of reason!

CHAPTER THREE

What Handwriting Analysis Cannot Reveal

Often a handwriting analyst returns a request to a client because graphology has its limitations and there are many things which cannot be revealed in the formations of handwriting. The client may misunderstand the purpose of graphology, and sometimes asks questions which are in the realm of prediction and guesswork (neither of which is part of handwriting analysis).

Here are some typical questions the graphologist receives:

"What does the future hold for me?" Naturally this cannot be answered, as surely no human being has the divine power to know what tomorrow will bring to anyone.

"I want to change my job, will the new one be successful for me?" First of all, the graphologist should be told the current job and the new job to which the person wants to change. Then, all the graphologist can do is to say which of the jobs might be best suited to the writer; but he certainly cannot promise success, as too many factors (other than the personality traits of the writer) may enter into the situation.

"Does this writing show a mental breakdown?" The writer is told to consult a physician, as it is not the function of a handwriting analyst to diagnose any ailment, either mental or physical. A graphologist may do clinical studies on handwritings with a psychiatrist or a physician, but he may not reach conclusive evidence of illness in the handwriting. This is still in the process of research, and the graphologist must never discuss illness in handwriting formations with a client.

"Am I the aggressive type?" A handwriting analyst does not work in "types," as each person is distinctly an individual. The formations may show the writer to be aggressive or to lack the aggressive trait; but as an individual and not as a "type."

"Why don't my neighbors like me?" In such a case, I should have the handwritings of the neighbors, to tell my client what each of these people is. Then she or he will know better how to understand the neighbors and perhaps be able to find out why there is no liking. Also, there may be some situations, aside from the inner personalities of these people, which might produce friction. So this, too, is in the guesswork category and the client may not be helped through handwriting analysis.

"Does he love me? Will he marry me?" No handwriting analyst can answer such queries. We do not read minds, or know what's in a person's heart. All that can be done is to analyze the handwriting and see if we can find his capacity to love someone, or if he might make good "marriage material." But further than that the graphologist cannot be of aid.

"My daughter is in college. Will she succeed in her studies?" If the graphologist is not told the subjects that are being studied, it is not possible to say if the student is qualified for such pursuits. And, even if potentially qualified, the handwriting analyst cannot promise success.

"Enclosed are the handwritings of three women. Which one should I marry?" All the graphologist can do is to give an analysis of each of the women, then tell the man he is the one to decide which of the three he thinks would be best for him.

"Is this a criminal handwriting?" While there are clinical graphologists who study the handwritings of criminals, with interesting results, the results are not too conclusive, because a person may be a kind and passive soul but in a moment of passion he might commit a crime. Or, a person may have violent tendencies, yet the situation might not arise (or that person might be strongly held in check by people of good influence), and so a crime may not be committed. Therefore, this is a question which a handwriting analyst cannot truly answer.

"We are a credit house. Will this customer, according to his handwriting, be a good risk and will he repay a loan?" This is interesting, as often the handwriting may show a person of sincerity and integrity who is a potential safe risk; yet a situation might arise where that sincere person may not be in a position to meet his obligations. Or, the handwriting may reveal someone who is potentially not a good risk; but he might repay a loan on time if he has the money or if he is scared his employer or his wife might find out about it. So, while the credit house may be wise in having the client's character analyzed, that firm cannot be promised that the loan will be repaid.

"I met this man, but I think he is married. Is he?" The graphologist cannot know, as handwriting does not reveal if a person is single or married. Marriage does not alter the basic traits of the individual, and the handwriting analysis is done only on the basic traits.

The foregoing is merely a sampling of the many queries which come to a handwriting analyst. The clients must be told that there is no such thing as guesswork, mind reading, or prediction connected with graphology.

Many requests come to a handwriting analyst regarding jobs and hobbies which people want to pursue, and they want an analysis to help them make their decisions. This phase of handwriting analysis is discussed in the following chapter.

AGE AND SEX NOT SHOWN IN HANDWRITING

When submitting a handwriting for analysis, the approximate age (birth date not necessary) and the sex of the writer should be told to the graphologist.

A person of fifty may have the naive attitudes or the intellectual stature of a person of fourteen, whereas a fourteen-year-old may have the sophisticated attitudes and mature intellect of one who is twice as old. In a handwriting the intellectual and emotional maturity or immaturity are shown (not the exact age). Thus, include the age of a person whenever requesting an analysis.

It is not possible to know if the writing is done by a man or a woman. If the specimen of handwriting is not accompanied by a full signature which signifies the writer's sex, the graphologist should be told. Often a letter is signed with initials only, or with a nickname which may be used by males and females (such as Pat, Jean, Lee, Buddy, etc.). A mother might write and say, "I enclose my child's writing," but does not specify if it's a male or female child. Some people say, "Here is the handwriting of my friend," but the graphologist has no way of knowing if it's a girl friend or boy friend.

A graphologist could make an analysis without knowing the sex and age, but it would be much fairer to the subject of the analysis if these factors were given to the handwriting analyst who could then give a more in-depth analysis.

FAMILY HANDWRITINGS NOT ALIKE

No, there is no such thing as a family handwriting! If any member of a family writes like another, it is merely a coincidence. A child might imitate the handwriting of a parent or other relative; but eventually that child's own handwriting will prevail (unless he or she is a chronic imitator and thus might even imitate other things that relative does). Not even identical twins write exactly alike. Each person in a family is a distinct individual, with his or her own innate personality, and the handwriting therefore is indicative of that individuality.

CHILDREN'S HANDWRITINGS

Unless the handwriting analyst is also trained in child psychology or other fields dealing with children, it is not easy to make an analysis of the handwriting of a very young child. In handling work through my own office, I may often return the handwriting of a very young child to a parent (or a teacher) who is requesting the analysis, asking that the handwriting be submitted to me later on when that child reaches age sixteen or is midway in high school. If the parent or teacher insists on the analysis, I do it, but I explain that it might be rather superficial if that child is still in the "developing" process both in mind and body.

Some children are "early bloomers" and some of them bloom late. A child may not have any manual dexterity and thus may take longer to acquire adeptness in writing. Thus, when I am asked "At what age can a child's handwriting be analyzed?" my answer is "Anywhere from six to sixteen, depending on the child."

Also there is the question of styles of penmanship. In the past twenty-five years many public and private schools have been teaching the first-graders the manuscript (block printing) style of penmanship. In some schools they still teach them the Palmer or a similar method, with the cursive, flowing, connected letter formations. Many children, who first learn the block printing penmanship, later on, from about age twelve up, start to do the cursive writing which is preferable for them.

Another factor is that when a child's family moves to another locality, or the child is transferred to another school, the style of penmanship taught may vary in the new school.

For example, there may be from twenty-five to forty-five pupils in one classroom, all taught the same penmanship method, all forced to produce that style of writing whether the individual child does or does not want to or is unable to follow it in precise manner. But the teacher insists every child must write the same, and this may persist for the entire eight years the pupil spends in primary school. However, despite the insistence of the teacher (often abetted by the parents) that each child write alike, some of the pupils just cannot do so. Take the handwritings of these same children a year, or five years, or ten years after they have graduated from primary school, and you will find many to be slightly or even completely different from the actual penmanship method they were taught to (and sometimes forced to) write. The individual personalities show through in the variations of the handwritings as these school children emerge into adulthood and are no longer under the discipline of the penmanship teacher.

Thus, it is part of the handwriting analyst's cautious judgment to be overly careful about analyzing a very young child's handwriting, as it may not yet be the final individual form which it will be when the child enters into the age of puberty.

In this book (which is for the layman, and not for the clinical analyst) I am not discussing children's handwritings separately. But there are books available which do contain information on research studies and developments in the field of children's behavior and handwritings; among them are: Klara Roman's *Handwriting—A Key to Personality,* and Hans J. Jacoby's *Analysis of Handwriting.*

CHAPTER FOUR

Does Handwriting Show Job Potentials?

A common question asked of the graphologist is, "Can you tell me what kind of work I do, through my handwriting?" The answer is in the negative, because often people are active in jobs, careers or professions, or hobbies, which might not show in the handwriting at all. If the person is intelligent and resourceful (and has the strong incentive of having to earn a living), he or she may do a very good job in some field for which the writing shows no aptitude at all. Some people have to grab the first job offered, or have to step into a family business (without free choice). So the graphologist cannot know what a person does, but he may be able to tell that person what the potentials are for certain paths of endeavor.

There is no such thing as the handwriting of a physician, secretary, lawyer, astronaut, butcher, musician, taxi driver, computer programmer, teacher, accountant, or any other field of work or profession. The job does not make the person! And the handwriting formations reveal the inner personality, regardless of the work the writer does. We will find stingy doctors and generous ones, gullible teachers and skeptical ones, introverted butchers and extroverted ones, so that we cannot say that any one personality trait or a combination of them in a handwriting applies to any one specific line of work.

Usually it takes a long period of study and practice in graphology before the analyst is capable of finding general work potentials in a handwriting, and helping to guide a person in the right direction. There are times when the handwriting does not pinpoint any work potentials toward which the graphologist might guide the client; in such case I frankly tell my client to seek the services of a professional vocational aptitude tester.

GENERAL JOB TENDENCIES SHOWN

In the following chapters you will find how to know if a person is intuitive or logical, critical or gullible, extroverted or introverted, and many other signs. Then, when trying to find work potentials or tendencies in a handwriting, the graphologist must know the requirements of a specific job. For instance, in a job where the person has to handle routine details and be interested in facts and figures (such as accountancy), the graphologist looks for signs in the handwriting which point up logical reasoning, ability to concentrate, emotional discipline, and whatever other factors there may be. Another example would be the person who wants to be a professional dancer or a sports figure. In this case the handwriting ought to show a flowing rhythm, preferably extroverted, large loops, heavy pressure, among other signs in the writing.

The foregoing two examples are sketchy, but they serve to show that the handwriting analyst does not look for a "doctor's handwriting" or a "cobbler's handwriting" but instead looks for many signs in the writing which the specific job or profession or hobby requires.

One might find in a handwriting the intellectual qualities a man needs to possess to become a scientist; but on the other hand these fine traits may be contradicted by adverse signs of lack of concentration, impatience, and other traits which would mitigate against that person's potential in the field of science.

Or, the graphologist may see in a handwriting many signs of sympathy and desire to help one's fellow beings, and the writer wants to become a nurse or a doctor or a Peace Corps worker. But, the other signs in the writing may offset these traits and show lack of sufficient ability to concentrate on the necessary studies for such fields of endeavor. The writing may show signs of gullibility; it may lack self-confidence which such work calls for. Thus, it would certainly not be wise for that person to pursue studies in a field that could hardly lead to fruition.

In such cases, where the handwriting analyst (after years of experience in personnel guiding through graphology) sees potentials for other work than the person wants to pursue, that advice will be suggested to the writer so that he or she may investigate the possibilities in other directions.

SCREENING JOB APPLICANTS

When the personnel director of a business firm or other organization submits handwritings to a graphologist, there is a procedure which should be followed in order to give the handwriting analyst as adequate a sample as possible to work on, and to be fair to the applicant as well as the employer.

Often a firm will send a printed application form, which is usually not a good sample from which to work. The applicant has to write on printed lines, usually in a small space; often he or she is asked to print (or prefers to print) for legibility on the form, and this may be entirely different from the natural handwriting which the applicant uses.

I suggest to such firms that they send me a sample of actual handwriting, in addition to or instead of the application form. Some of them subtly leave the whole or half of the last page of the form blank, and instruct the applicant to write (in his natural handwriting) a sample sales letter or whatever other theme is relative to the job which is offered. And it is from this handwritten portion, on unlined paper, that the graphologist can do a better and much fairer analysis.

The employer also sends the graphologist the job requirement specifics. If he just says "salesman" or "manager" or "clerk," the handwriting analyst does not really know what the employer requires his employee to do on the job. In addition, the employer usually tells the handwriting analyst what kind of person he wants for each particular job; one firm might want an extrovert in a certain job, whereas another firm might prefer a more reserved person in a similar position.

A graphologist does not tell an employer "Do hire this one" or "Don't hire this one," because there may be some other factors involved, apart from personality traits, which might make the applicant desirable or not desirable for that particular firm. But the analysis is made with the specific job in mind and what traits the employer seeks in the employee. Sometimes the handwriting analyst might suggest that an applicant might be better suited to a different department in that firm's organization, if the signs in the handwriting do not point specifically toward suitability for the specific job the employer is offering.

Some firms, at "shifting around" time when they want to promote or transfer some of their employees, avail themselves of a handwriting analyst in the same manner as when interviewing job applicants.

Handwriting analysis is usually not the only testing device used in personnel screening; many firms use a battery of psychological tests and consider graphology as the supplemental tool.

CHAPTER FIVE

National Handwriting Styles

The basic rules of analysis of handwriting apply to the various styles of penmanship taught in European countries, in this country, and all others writing with the letter formations which are used in the Western world and which came down to us through the Babylonians, Egyptians, Cretes, Hittites, Phoenicians, Greeks, and Romans. In the different nations as they evolved, some changes did come into the original writing forms, until now we can usually look at a person's handwriting and know if the origin of that penmanship comes from England or Spain or Russia, or some other country. But this does not mean that the writer himself was born in that country. It signifies that his teacher comes from that country or learned to write in that country. Thus, it is not possible for any graphologist to be able to answer the often asked question, "Can you tell me where this person was born, according to the handwriting?"

A person might be a native of Spain, for example, but could have come to the United States as a child and attended school here; that handwriting is an "American hand" and may not show any traces of a Spanish background. Or, an American-born child may be taken to Italy and taught to write in an Italian school, without showing any traces of his American birth in his handwriting. Human nature is the same regardless of the country of birth, and the personality traits are inherent in the man or woman regardless of the place of birth or later upbringing.

VARYING PENMANSHIP STYLES IN DIFFERENT COUNTRIES

The Italian handwriting usually contains flowing capital letters showing much romance and gaiety. Often these large capitals are accompanied by small, lower-case letters in rhythmic flow over the page, which may show precision in handwork as well as music.

French writing generally shows meticulous letter formations. They are usually small and clear, and the capital letters are not exaggerated in size. This may show cool and logical thinking, and fine sensibilities.

The Spanish writing usually contains ornate capital letters, signifying a stately pride. The small letters are generally connected with long strokes, expressing rhythm and a response to beauty.

In the German writing we find more intricate letter forms, which usually show careful and detailed thinking. The German script is usually more angular than the American handwriting.

Russian handwriting usually contains long connecting strokes between the letters, large ornamented capital letters, and the rhythm of the writing is rather a sprawling one. These point to garrulity and outgoing personality traits.

In England, Ireland, Scotland, and Wales (and other countries which are part of the British Commonwealth) we find they write in a similarity of penmanship style. The handwriting is usually more vertical than the American, and shows a clannish instinct.

In our own country we do not have one penmanship style, so it is hard to point to any one handwriting and say it is an American script. The forward-leaning cursive writing (known as the Palmer method, or by other names in certain areas) is about as indigenous to the vital American national attitude as we can get. But in the past two or three decades our schools have introduced the manuscript (block printing) style of penmanship, and this new style has made deep inroads into the vital cursive letter forms. Also, many Americans are deeply influenced by the nationality of their forebears and there may creep into the American penmanship some signs of British, Spanish, German, and other nationalities. This makes the American handwriting very interesting to analyze, as there is no such thing as "an American style."

While the Hebrew, Turkish, Arabic, and other handwritings from that area of the world are different in letter forms from the handwritings of the Western world, they did start originally from the same source. It is amazing how a trained graphologist is able to observe similar personality signs in those handwritings as far as size, width, pressure, and horizontal and vertical lines are concerned.

Chinese and Japanese handwritings are, however, not within the scope of the American or European graphologist, unless that handwriting analyst has studied those oriental "picture styles" of penmanship. However, there are undoubtedly handwriting analysts in those Far East countries who are able to practice their own native graphological rules.

Just as fashions change in clothes and home decorations, so do penmanship fashions follow the trends. Basically the personality traits of people do not change, so the basic handwriting signs do not change; but the fashion does change in a more or less superficial manner.

For example, in the eighteenth century in this country it was fashionable to make adornments on the capital letters, to underscore signatures with graceful but conspicuous lines, and in some cases you will find the small letter "s" written the same way as the letter "f" is done.

Later, in the nineteenth century, when women wore bustles and exaggerated trimmings and puffed-out sleeves, there was a certain "heaviness" in home furnishings too. During this period in this country the Spencerian style of handwriting developed; it was done with beautiful shading of the lower letters and capitals, and one was greatly admired who could write "a beautiful hand."

It is interesting to note that certain modes of clothes, home furnishings, and even social-life activities, all had their effect on the manners of the time, and when it was considered most elegant to be over-dressed and have pompous manners, the handwriting (the Spencerian style) also took on the spirit of the time.

Now we come to this century, to current times, when fashion in clothes strips off all trimmings considered to be nonessential, when homes are stripped of as many decorations as are regarded to be overbearing, and when conventional social-life amenities are not observed in the way they used to be. People seem to strip themselves not only as far as clothes and homes and activities are concerned, but in their handwritings as well. Gone are the flourishes of the eighteenth and nineteenth centuries!

Yet, to the trained graphologist the stripping of nonessential curlicues from the handwriting does not really alter the basic traits which are seen in the writing formations. Fashions come and go, but basic values remain—in handwriting as well as in all other things touching people's lives.

CHAPTER SIX

How to Prepare to Make an Analysis

The trained handwriting analyst may be able to make an analysis of a specimen of writing which is not ideally suited to the purpose; but no matter how long the experience of the graphologist there may still be some handwriting samples which are not fair samples for purposes of analysis.

The ideal specimen is for the handwriting to be written on a full sheet of paper, which has no printed lines on it and no printed margins. When the paper has these printed lines, it is difficult for the handwriting analyst to know whether the person writes with the lines going uphill or downhill on the page, also whether the margins are wide and narrow.

An addressed envelope (often such a specimen is given to a graphologist for analysis) is not a fair sample, as there is no way of knowing how that person slants and spaces full sentences or how he makes margins.

Poetry, too, is not too fair a sample, as here also the natural spacing and margins cannot be seen.

It is best to have handwriting which is done in a spontaneous manner; not dictated to the writer, and not copied from a book or magazine. Dictation or copying may slow up the natural speed of the handwriting, and may cause the handwriting to be stilted and not in its natural speed and rhythm.

In recent years the photocopy has become a popular way of handling papers, especially in business offices. While the trained graphologist may be able to do the analysis from a photocopy, it is best to see the original handwriting (if possible) as the copy is not always too clear. This also applies to facsimiles of handwritings which may appear in newspapers.

A signature alone is not usually analyzed, because in many cases the name is signed in a handwriting that is not exactly like the body of the writing. Some people devise certain stylized signatures, to be different, to assert their individuality or ego. Therefore, if a graphologist makes an analysis of a signature only, the client is told that it may not be a completely true picture of the personality. A few lines of handwriting should accompany the signature. However, a specimen of writing alone (without the signature) is appropriate for purposes of analysis.

DETAILS TO ACCOMPANY HANDWRITING

As said before, an experienced handwriting analyst may be able to work on any sample of writing. But for best results, especially in helping the client, it is necessary to have some details aside from the writing itself. For example, the graphologist should be told the approximate age of the writer, also whether the sample is from a male or female.

If the client wants the graphologist to give suggestions as to a job or profession or hobby which might be pursued, the handwriting analyst should be told what the client's work or hobby is, or what he may be desirous of doing. The graphologist cannot read minds or do any guessing. So if any specific details are wanted by the client he should give specific reasons why the analysis is desired. Otherwise, the analysis can be only on the general basic traits. It is as if one went to a physician and did not tell the symptoms which prompted the patient to seek aid. The more details the graphologist can have, when the client wants specific suggestions in addition to a general analysis, the better the handwriting analyst can serve the client.

A person might write and want to know about other people in his life (in his home, or social or business matters). In such a case, it is necessary that the handwriting of each of the people involved be submitted to the handwriting analyst, with specific details given about each person. It is not possible to analyze anybody else, from the client's handwriting alone.

A graphologist may receive a request, such as, "I want to see if I have changed in the last five years, when I had an analysis made of my handwriting." In such a case the current sample of writing is not enough for a basis of comparison. The client should be asked to send along a sample of the writing of five years ago, also if possible to send along the previous analysis. Only then is it possible to make a comparison and see if any changes or developments did take place.

A client may say, "My handwriting changed ever since I got a job as a typist. The typewriter ruined my handwriting." Or, a stenographer will often say, "Since I studied shorthand I don't write as beautifully as I used to do." Yes, their handwritings may show changes, but the reasons they express are not valid. The changes (or developments) take place in the handwriting as the person matures, and they have nothing to do with the job he or she performs or the tools which the person uses. A typewriter, a stenotype machine, an adding or other business machine, is merely a tool of the trade, just the way a bricklayer handles his trowel or a carpenter his hammer. But, when the day's work is done, and the tool is laid aside, the handwriting is expressive of the inner personality and has nothing to do with the job or the tools used in its performance.

MISLEADING SITUATIONS

The handwriting of a famous person always shows to the graphologist what the inner traits of that person really are. A prominent man or woman in the theatre or politics or other outstanding fields may present a most forceful personality to the public; yet the handwriting may show (to the trained graphologist) the signs of introversion and perhaps many gentle traits which are hidden from the public. Thus, when examining the handwriting of a famous person, the graphologist needs to forget the public image and most objectively study the handwriting formations which portray the inner personality.

A physician's prescription blank may be sent to a graphologist for purposes of analysis; but the cautious analyst will not make the deductions from that blank alone and will ask to see a sample of writing in the doctor's natural penmanship. The doctor may write illegibly on his prescription blank, because it seems to be a matter of professional prestige or legend to do so. Of course, the physician's natural handwriting may be just like the prescription blank; but just on the chance that it is not, it is better not to analyze the latter without having some additional handwriting.

Sometimes a sheet of figures is sent to the graphologist. In themselves figures alone are not too good a sample on which to work; the numbers should be accompanied by a sample of writing. Usually the numbers are the same as the handwriting, in size and spacing and pressure; but it is not recommended that a graphologist proceed with an analysis only from figures.

Engineers, architects, draftsmen, commercial artists, librarians, and keepers of records are usually taught to print in connection with their jobs. But this does not mean that they write their personal letters with printed formations (unless the trained graphologist finds it is more natural for the person to print than to make cursive forms, according to certain inner traits). These people may use cursive writing in their personal letters or reports. The graphologist should therefore be given a sample of their actual handwritings and not merely the work sheets with printing. It may not be fair to the writer, or to the handwriting analyst, to work only from printing done on work sheets or blueprints.

When a client says, "But I have three different kinds of handwriting," he should be asked to submit a sample of the different styles of his penmanship. It should not take the trained graphologist long to know which is the basic handwriting and why the variations take place in the different styles.

FOREIGN LANGUAGES

Often it is necessary to make some allowances in the differences of the letter forms between an American writing and a foreign one. For instance, the German script is usually more angular than the writing in this country, so the graphologist makes certain allowances and may discount some of the angles.

If English is the second language of some people; that is, if they first learned Spanish or some other language, then came to this country and learned English (or studied it as a second language in their own country), the handwriting analyst should ask to see a sample of the writing done in the first language the writer learned as well as a sample done in English. Usually there will be no real difference; but there is a chance that the English (the later language) may be written in a more labored manner and not be in as natural a rhythm as the client's original language. In such case the graphologist has to pay strict attention to the first language and not rely entirely on that written in English.

An interesting thing, along this same line, is that when the manuscript (block printing) style of penmanship started to be taught in the American schools, the handwriting analysts had to cope with new formations, and the way to do this was by regarding the manuscript writing in the same way one analyzes a foreign language. The graphologist studies pressure, size, slant, spacing, etc., until the manuscript writing is understood in the same way that the regular cursive handwriting can be handled.

MAKING AN ANALYSIS

When you have familiarized yourself with the following chapters which describe the fundamental rules of handwriting analysis, you may want to make your first test.

It might be a good idea to start on a sample of your own handwriting, and then go on to the writings of others.

The prime thing you must possess, when starting an analysis, is complete objectivity! You may not like a certain person, or may judge some of his traits (faults as well as virtues) from the way that person acts. Yet, you must not permit your attitude to be prejudiced, and your approach to an analysis of a handwriting must be devoid of all personal feeling.

You may be given a sample of writing which is done on expensive stationery; but this does not necessarily mean the writer has good taste (the paper might have been a birthday gift). Or, you may see handwriting done on a scrap of paper or inexpensive stationery; here, too, you cannot judge the person on that score, as this may be someone of excellent taste but whose writing was done hurriedly with no thought given to the stylishness of the paper.

Also do not always judge by the text of what is written: some people deliberately write things to "put the graphologist off." The exception here is that when the person includes detailed information relating to the analysis (such as the work or studies or other things which he wants the handwriting analyst to answer), then the text of the letter is taken into consideration by the graphologist.

If you get a few sheets of writing from one person, a good idea is to analyze the last sheet and work forward, because when the writer starts on the first page, it may be a bit stilted; but when the writing gets to the following pages, it flows more freely and the writer is not so self-conscious. If you have one sheet of writing to work on, start at the bottom and then examine the writing upward, as the same applies here. In some cases the person may be inhibited when starting to write a letter, or a sheet of composition, or a report; but he gains confidence as he proceeds, and so the end of the written matter may be much freer than its beginning.

Do not presume to give advice or suggestions about a person's suitability for a certain job or study unless you know something about it. For instance, if someone says he wants to be a tree surgeon, or if a girl wants to be an occupational therapist, it is obligatory for the graphologist to get some information on such jobs before anything can be said in the analysis to indicate whether the client does or does not have potentials for such chosen fields. Therefore, it behooves the beginner graphologist to avoid such specific advice to clients; he should spend much time in general analysis of the traits of character until enough experience and training is gained to broaden his endeavors. While handwriting analysis is able to show personality traits and potential work abilities, it is still only an auxiliary tool in psychological testing, and the beginner in the field must realize its limitations and never shirk its responsibilities.

In examining a specimen of writing, use a magnifying glass (a small one is good enough) so you may see the various forms of "i" dots or little hooks at beginning and end of strokes, or variations in pressure.

Provide yourself with a pad, on which you may write headings such as: Size, Pressure, Spaces between words, Spaces between letters, Spaces between lines, Margins, "t" crossings, "i" dots, and the many other signs in writing which are discussed in the following chapters.

Write down what you observe in the examination of the

handwriting specimen; for instance, you might say "small" under Size, or "wide" under Spaces between lines, and the many other signs you discover.

Then see how many similarities you find, or how many contradictions appear. No one handwriting provides all signs pointing to a similar conclusion, so you then have to do "adding, substracting, dividing, and multiplying" of all the signs you found in the handwriting. If, for instance, a certain loop (in an "l" or a "g") never varies, then you know it is consistent with a certain personality trait the writer possesses. But if you find three long "t" bars, which usually mean an enterprising person; then you also discover eight "t" bars which do not go through the vertical stem of the letter, you know that person has a strong streak of procrastination. Putting the two together, you may surmise that while the writer is enthusiastic (those long "t" bars) he may not follow through because of his procrastination (those halfway "t" bars).

The foregoing procedure must be repeated over and over again, in your study of the various formations in the handwriting, until you finally arrive at a synthesis of all your findings and are able to construct the total personality therefrom.

STUDYING VARIOUS SIGNS IN HANDWRITING

It is quite likely that you may find in a specimen of handwriting some strange sign or a combination of signs which is not discussed in the following chapters. This happens to the most experienced professional graphologist. Each person is a distinct individual, with his or her own traits of virtues and/or faults, and occasionally you may

Trinidad High
School Library

find a unique handwriting formation belonging to a unique person. When the graphologist comes across such a situation, the unfamiliar sign is studied in relation to all other graphological signs in the handwriting rather than stressed too strongly by itself.

You may be shocked at the results of your first analysis, either of your own handwriting or that of another person; you may not fully recognize the "personality picture" which the analysis produces. But, objectively, you will soon learn that the outer personality is not always expressive of the inner one, and a handwriting analysis brings to the surface many hidden traits which were not previously recognized by you or by the other person who was the subject of the analysis.

MIRROR HANDWRITING

If the neophyte graphologist is given a handwriting which is done entirely backward, or upside down, on the sheet of paper, the wise thing is not to attempt making an analysis. Of course you may hold the sample of writing up to a mirror and find that its reflection gives you the normal state of a handwriting. Yet, there may be some underlying cause why the person writes in this manner; it may be an eye condition which should be diagnosed by an ophthalmologist; or some other situation which is not within the province of a handwriting analyst to tackle.

Mirror writing more often occurs in the handwriting of a child, than in an adult. If you come across such a case, it is best to suggest the person discuss the unusual style of handwriting with a psychologist.

DISGUISED HANDWRITING

Occasionally a graphologist is given a sample of writing which is disguised, and is not the natural script of that person. Sometimes this is done deliberately, at other times it may be just a prank to befuddle the handwriting analyst. The trained graphologist is usually able to discern that the handwriting was not written in a natural, spontaneous manner. It is not possible to specifically tell here how one is able to discover the disguises in the handwriting (and the novice graphologist will hardly be expected to be able to recognize it); but generally the experienced handwriting analyst will find formations which are not compatible with the rest of the handwriting. For example, there are capital letters which are too conspicuous, or loops in such letters as "f" and "g" may be exaggerated, and some of the downstrokes in the letters have conspicuously heavier pressures than the upward strokes.

It is not really easy for anyone to write a completely disguised handwriting; but this situation does occur once in a while. So the student of handwriting analysis should be made aware of it.

WRITING UNDER HYPNOSIS

Experiments are made with people who are under hypnotic suggestion, and they are asked to write as they did when they were children, or at other times of their lives. This is still in the stage of clinical research, and some interesting results are often shown but are not yet conclusive in their acceptance in the field of graphology. This may eventually produce more effective results, with longer study; but the beginner graphologist should be cautious if asked to make an analysis of writing produced in a state of hypnosis.

CHAPTER SEVEN

Slants of Handwriting

The most common form of handwriting slants toward the right. But many people write in a definite backhand manner (the letters slanting toward the left), and some write in a vertical manner that is straight up-and-down and does not go in either a rightward or leftward direction. And there are handwritings which go in every direction. All of these are significant when making an analysis of handwriting.

There is a tendency on the part of the layman to think that because a handwriting is backhand (toward the left in slant) it is written by a left-handed person. Recently, while watching a television show depicting a fictional detective story, I heard the actor say, "We now have a clue; this was written by a left-handed person because it is backhand." Naturally I dispatched a letter to the director of that show pointing out the fallacious statement and suggesting he engage the service of a handwriting analyst whenever one of the incidents in the shows referred to a diagnosis of handwriting formations.

Whether the writer uses his right hand or his left hand, the movements of his pen or pencil will depict the inner personality traits; thus, it is difficult (or perhaps impossible) for the graphologist to know which hand holds the pen. Some left-hand writers find it necessary to turn the sheet of paper in a different position than the one who uses his right hand. But the end result of the handwriting is not affected by this. A graphologist might ask a client if the writing is done with either the left or the right hand; but this is merely as a statistic or for some matter of further research, and not because the backhand slant or any other sign of the handwriting indicates left-handedness.

FORWARD, BACKHAND, VERTICAL WRITING

This simple chart enables the analyst to measure the degree of the slants of handwriting. Make a tracing of this chart and lay the tracing on top of the handwriting specimen so you may see the angle of the slant.

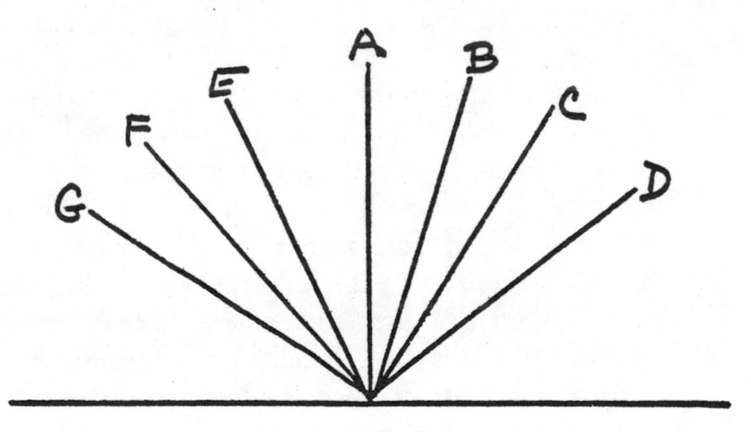

Generally, slant A indicates emotional control, good balance between head and heart. Slants B, C, and D are regarded as the extroverted signs, and these writers like to look forward to new things. Slants E, F, and G are written by people who may be inclined to hold back, even to look back to the past and be hesitant to take a forward step, and they are usually introverts.

More specifically, the following is the way these directions of handwriting are analyzed. However, just because several samples of writing slant in the same direction, it does not mean they all have the same meaning, as they may have various differences in other signs of the handwriting.

A—When this vertical writing consists of small, even letters, with proportional small capitals, and a light pressure of the pen, it shows the writer to be reserved in manner and to prefer a well-organized life and no taking of unnecessary risks. The physical appetites are subdued.

Vertical handwriting which has rounded formations, medium size letters, well-formed medium capitals, and "t" crossing bars which are short, inconspicuous lines, reveals the person to be interested in the welfare of other people. There is no pretense in the personality makeup. This writer's love is usually expressed in a young, sentimental manner rather than maturely romantic.

If the upright writing is done with a heavy pressure of the pen, the formations narrow and angular (points where rounded forms should normally appear), the personality it portrays is one that is not warmly inclined toward other people. All tasks are done in an efficient manner, and the mind is usually the dominant factor when decisions must be made.

B—This is the most common slant shown in handwritings. It shows friendliness, ability to show the affections, a desire to function cooperatively with others.

C—Here is a more assertive character, and more individualistic than B. There may be strong sex attraction here; if the pressure of the pen is very heavy, it shows sensuality; but if the pressure is very light, the feelings of sex may be more idealistic (although strong, as the angle indicates).

D—The more extreme angle of writing shows an emotional person, one who may not entirely be physically ardent but who may be so in imagination. The lighter the pressure of the pen, the more imaginative the person may be. The writer with this extreme slant is intense, and all things are expressed in an emotional manner.

E—This backhand slant of writing reveals a person who is reserved, who may be inhibited and self-conscious, and may hold back from expression of individualistic ideas. The mind usually controls the heart. The various other signs in the handwriting have to be taken into consideration when making the analysis.

F—This backward slant (or the G slant that may be even more extreme) is merely an intensification of the E writing. This person is not too easy to understand, because of his drawing back from others to a great extent.

VARIABLE SLANTS

The following illustration shows handwriting which normally slants to the right, yet some of the letters (usually the ones with loops) are pulled backhand. This departure from the norm has to be carefully studied to determine why this "pulling back" takes place.

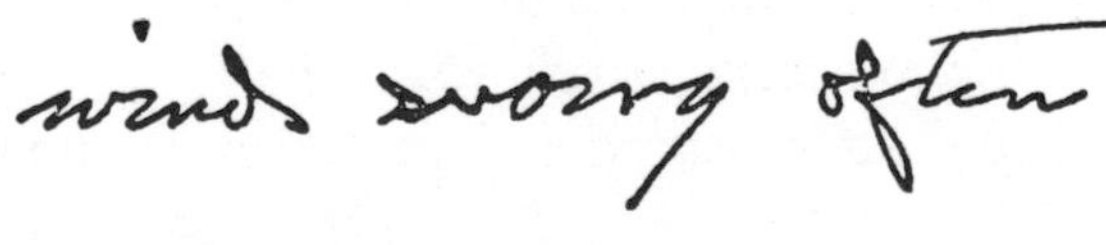

This shows the writer may be hesitant or afraid to go forward in meeting new people, ideas, and situations; there is uncertainty in the way of thinking, and this person may be hard to know and hard to please. The writer may sometimes fuss over nonessentials and make life more difficult than it really needs to be.

Handwriting which is done with variable slants, either in one word, or a line, or a whole page of writing, shows emotional youngness, regardless of the chronological age of the writer. The head and the heart are usually in conflict; the mind may dictate the person go in one direction, but the heart (the emotions) may pull him some other way. Instead of solving the situation right away, this person is apt to go through a continual inner turmoil between mind and emotions. If the handwriting shows strength in other ways (good strong "t" bars, heavy pressure, and other signs of self-confidence), then this emotionalism may not be a constant weakness, and it might only be a sign of variable moods which may change according to fluctuating situations. A writer who keeps on changing the slants of writing all the time is one who doesn't like to be tied down to routine, and may get bored with details and with people and surroundings if they seem to be too static to him.

When a person is able to write two or more different kinds of handwriting, in different slants, and each sample of the writing is clear and not "emotionally varied" as discussed in the foregoing paragraph, then the graphologist knows the person wants to be "all things to all men" and is able to put on an act and consciously play the right part and give the best performance according to the particular situation. However, the trained handwriting analyst will usually find the same *basic* personality traits in the different styles of writing.

SIGNATURES SLANT DIFFERENTLY

In a specimen of handwriting you may find the signature slants in a different angle from the rest of the writing. This is not to be regarded merely as a "variable slant," as it may have deeper significance. Please refer to Chapter XIX for a fuller discussion on the subject of signatures.

COMPLETE CHANGE OF SLANT

A child may be taught the Palmer or similar method of penmanship which insists on a forward-leaning handwriting which slants to the right. Or, a child may attend a school where the manuscript (block printing) method of penmanship is taught, and this usually has no slant at all but is done in a vertical manner.

The child, on entering adulthood, may think and express himself or herself in an individualistic manner, in accordance with the basic personality. This is the time of the child's "declaration of independence" and, when no longer under the domination of the penmanship teacher, the handwriting may change completely, especially the slant. The one who wrote with forward-leaning formations may now write backhand (if that person is a natural introvert); the one who was taught to write with vertical strokes may now write in a forward-leaning angle (if that person is a natural extrovert).

Therefore, when an adolescent changes the slant of the handwriting, it must not be considered merely as a "variable slant" but should be analyzed from the viewpoint of the angle of writing which is followed by the writer at this point. It is often a matter of wonderment (sometimes even apprehension) to a young person who finds the handwriting slant has changed considerably. But the analyst can easily explain it as the natural "growing up" process and assertion of individual traits.

CHAPTER EIGHT

Base Line of Writing

When the child is given its first lesson in penmanship, paper with printed horizontal lines is used in order to guide the child in writing straight across the sheet. Later on the child discards the ruled sheet and starts to write without any guideline. At first this may be difficult, and some children may need a year or two to get accustomed to writing across the sheet without the help of the printed line. The handwriting analyst must take this into consideration when the writing is from a young person.

Some adults never seem to be able to write on a blank sheet of paper: they still must use a sheet with printed lines or put a guideline sheet under the paper and write over that. In such a case it causes a hardship to the graphologist, as it is not always possible to determine how that person may have written without such guidelines.

The handwriting analyst must try in every case to procure a specimen of writing done on plain paper, to see whether the person naturally writes with an ascending or a descending line, or writes straight across, or has a base line that varies in all directions.

THE STRAIGHT, EVEN BASE LINE

When the writing has a base line which runs straight

across the page (without the aid of printed lines or an under-sheet of guideline paper), the writer is generally well-controlled and is able to keep the moods on an even keel.

Of course, the graphologist must also study the various signs in the handwriting; if the letter formations are rounded and even, with an even pressure of the pen, the writer does not have any difficulty in maintaining a serene attitude toward life and its people.

But if the writing with the straight base line shows variations in letter formations, uneven pressure, angular rather than rounded letters, it may signify the person is not naturally calm but is able to discipline himself so he can maintain an outer attitude of calmness in dealing with others and in facing the facts of life.

Here is shown a handwriting which has a square look at the bottom of each letter as it rests on the base line. This is obviously achieved by using a guideline sheet under the page on which the writing is done.

not natural line

In this case, the handwriting analyst must not put too much stress on the base line, but proceed with the analysis based on the findings of all other signs in the handwriting.

ASCENDING AND DESCENDING BASE LINES

Generally, writing which is done with an ascending base line reveals optimism. In reverse, writing which has a descending base line shows pessimism or skepticism.

1. ascending

2. descending

3. variation in base line

4. each goes again

5. once again here

6. this is not straight

7. this is not straight

1. Should the uphill base line be only at a slight angle, the tendency to optimism is good and this person is usually in a cheery mood.

But, if the ascending base line is at too extreme an angle, it may indicate the writer has an inclination to exaggerate the optimism and may often be too buoyant in spirit and not sufficiently realistic.

When the uphill writing is made with large capital letters and widespread small letters, this person has an expansive nature and sometimes is able to sway others to become optimistic as well. The optimism may not always be founded on sound judgment, but it is a strong part of the personality makeup, and it cannot be easily squelched even in the face of disappointment.

2. The downhill writing shows the person who is prone to pessimism. If the descending base line is only slightly downhill, it may merely be a temporary reflection of the person's fatigue and not be a true sign of a pessimistic nature. For that reason it may be a good idea, with a sample of writing that runs downhill, to ask the person to show a sample or two of his handwriting done yesterday or a week ago, and it might show a straight or even ascending base line (which would indicate this pessimism is just a transient thing).

But, if the descent of the base line is done with an extreme slant, it shows an intensification of the explanation in the foregoing paragraph. This writer may give in too easily to moments of pessimism.

If a downhill handwriting has long, strong "t" crossing bars, and the writing is clear and well-formed, the pessimistic state of mind may not be too deep. But, if the writing is rather disorganized with letter formations of all sizes, with variable slants going to the right or backhand, then the trait of pessimism is more pronounced.

An unusual base line is sometimes seen in a handwriting that goes straight across the sheet, and suddenly at the end of the line (the last word ending) the base line drops down. The writer who does this must be carefully judged, because while his outer manner may give people the impression that he is a well-disciplined and calm person, beneath the surface there may lurk a strong tendency to pessimism and skepticism.

VARIATIONS IN BASE LINE

3. Not all base lines are straight or consistently uphill or downhill; sometimes there are many variations in the base line. When the words seem to float around, rather than be based on any definite line, sometimes uphill and other times downhill, it shows the person has variable moods and will be alternately optimistic or pessimistic depending on the fluctuation of his own moods. This might be caused by a temporary situation, of course, and it might be well to ask for a sample of writing done previously by the same person. But, if this is the way the writing always appears, it indicates the writer might be a very interesting companion, as he is often a puzzlement because of the variability of his moods and interests. This writer doesn't like routine and becomes impatient with anything or anyone that threatens to tie him down in any way.

4. Words may be written in a steplike manner, the beginning of the word starting down on the base line and the end of the word way above it. This is usually the sign

of a person who may overreach in optimism but not have the capacity to follow through, thus pulling back to reality and starting all over again. This is the writing of the day-dreaming optimist rather than the realistic one.

5. When the steplike words are written in a descending manner, they reveal the person whose natural tendency is toward pessimism, yet has a strong desire to overcome such an attitude and keeps trying to come out on top, though he may not be able to do so. The outer manner may not betray to others the inner conflict against pessimism.

6. The base line of a handwriting may appear to be straight across, yet when the handwriting analyst draws a line under it, there appears a convex shape. In such a case the writer starts out with a good deal of optimistic aim, but if results are not forthcoming very soon, the interest may lag and the person may lose his optimism about that certain desired result.

7. If, when drawing a line under the base line of handwriting, the analyst finds it to be a concave shape (and not actually straight across as it seemed to be), this tells a story that is quite different from the one in Item 6. Here the writer may start a new project with little self-confidence and not enough optimism; but as he proceeds he may see promise of a successful result and then his faith in himself is renewed and pessimism is overcome.

CHAPTER NINE

Margin Widths

When your eye glances at a framed etching or drawing hung on the wall, unconsciously you respond to its good taste by the way it is framed and this usually means there are wide margins (matting) around the drawing. The frame is not placed directly onto the drawing itself, as that would detract from its ultimate charm. In the same way the sheet of paper with handwriting on it gives the impression of good placement when tasteful, wide margins appear between the handwriting and the outer edges of the paper.

Sometimes a specimen of writing is submitted on paper which has a printed left-hand margin running vertically down the sheet. This is often used by accountants or by other business people. In such a case the analyst is unable to determine the actual margin placement, and he may need to ignore it and just make the analysis from the various other signs in the handwriting. This printed margin may prevent the writer from showing the natural margins which would otherwise be used on a page of handwriting.

If the handwriting to be analyzed is written on a postcard, or a small piece of paper (taken out of an address book, etc.), it might be best not to judge the margins at all.

Many people who write large and make wide margins may have to cramp the size in writing within the small area of the card. Thus it would not be fair, either to the subject whose handwriting is being analyzed or to the graphologist, to try and read the meaning in margins which might not be a true indication of the natural spacing on a regular-sized sheet of paper.

When wide margins are made around the four sides of the handwriting (left and right side of sheet, also top and bottom of sheet), it indicates the writer to be a person of good taste and to have an appreciation of things of artistic value. The writer may not be able to do any work of an artistic nature, but the ability to appreciate it is shown in wide margins.

MARGINS ON LEFT SIDE AND RIGHT SIDE OF SHEET

The left margin is more important than the others, as it is the point where the writer has to place the pen and pencil to start writing the whole line, and the place where the pen has to be brought back on each succeeding line to start the writing again.

The right margin is not as significant as the left margin, as sometimes the writer might go way over to the edge of the paper if he is writing a long word and does not wish to hyphenate it. Or, sometimes the person does not want to start to use another sheet and prefers to do all the writing on one sheet, and so he may consciously crowd the right margin. However, this will be discussed in the following paragraphs to show its relationship to the left margin.

As told previously in this chapter, wide margins on both sides show good taste and artistic appreciation; they may also show generosity in the handling of finances.

A wide margin on the left bears out this desire for fine

things and for spending; but if the right margin is narrow, it shows ability to curb any extravagance which the writer cannot afford.

When the left margin is narrow (or almost nonexistent), it shows the writer wants to be cautious in the handling of money; if the right margin is just as narrow, then the person knows how to get best results in return for expenditures, and has a good sense of thrift regarding saving for the future.

But, when the narrow left margin is accompanied by a wide right margin, then the desire to be thrifty is sometimes overcome by spurts of generosity; however, that narrow left margin shows the person always pulls back to his innate thriftiness.

People whose left and right margins are of different widths may show other signs of inner conflict in the handwriting, to back up this conflict which they have between thrifty and generous handling of finances.

VARIABILITY IN MARGIN WIDTHS

A person may start a letter with a narrow left margin, but as the writing proceeds down the sheet that margin gradually tapers until it is much wider at the bottom of the sheet (the last line of handwriting) than at its beginning. This usually indicates that the writer is consciously trying to practice thrift (so the margin starts narrow), but the natural generous nature cannot be inhibited and so it asserts itself (in the wider space at the bottom margin).

When the reverse appears; that is, when the left margin is very wide at the top of the sheet of writing but tapers down until it becomes a narrow margin at the bottom of the paper (the last line of writing), this shows the writer has an inner conflict between his natural trait of thrift (the narrow margin at the bottom) and the occasional desire to be more generous (shown in the wide margin at the top of the page). However, as the analysis is made by starting at the bottom of the sheet and working upward (as told in Chapter VI), the handwriting analyst knows that the writer is careful with money, even though he might make a show of occasionally being a spender.

If margins are wide, but made in a disorderly and uneven manner, they may reveal the person to have some feeling for beauty, but at the same time to have poor judgment. Narrow, disorderly margins bear out poor judgment too, without necessarily having the good taste to go along with it.

AFFECTATIONS IN MARGINS

When the lines of handwriting are placed in some highly original manner on the sheet of paper, for instance, at an angle of forty-five degrees as shown in this illustration:

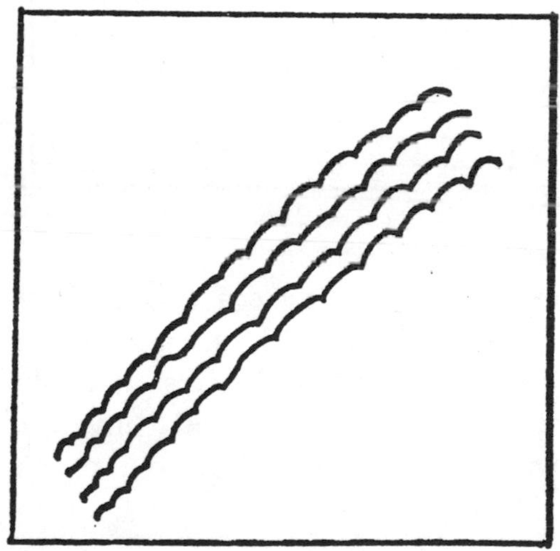

it reveals the person is trying to create an impression on other people and wants to be "different" from the ordinary run-of-the-mill person. Of course the graphologist may find, in the analysis of the formations of handwriting, other signs of making a bid for attention. But this is not a usual specimen as far as margins are concerned, and in making the analysis the rules concerning these factors may need to be disregarded.

Another way of individualistic spacing of the lines of writing is shown:

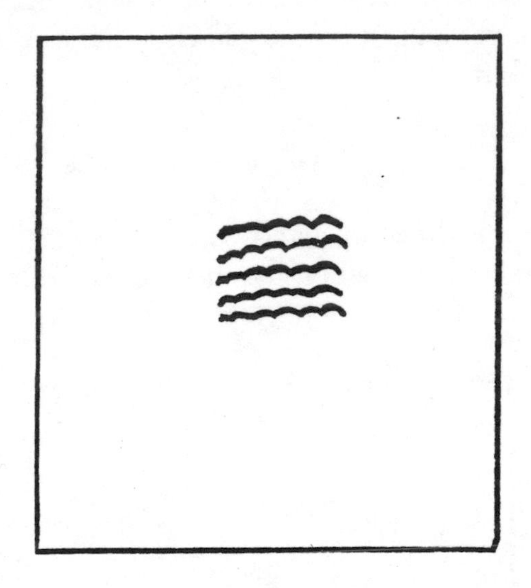

Here too we may have to disregard the rules of analyzing margins and find the clue to this person's character by studying the formations themselves. It might show an introspective person who puts himself into a solitary spot away from others; or it may signify a person of much artistic taste; or perhaps this writer wants to create a big impression on others.

The foregoing two examples are shown merely as exaggerations of margins; they may not be able to be fitted into general categories.

CHAPTER TEN

Spacing between Lines, Words, Letters

A popular fallacy is that large handwriting shows generosity while small writing reveals stinginess. Actually the attitude about spending or hoarding money is seen in the width or narrowness of the spacing between words and lines of writing, and not in the size of the letters. A person might write very large, yet have no spaces between words and lines, and this would show a thrifty soul. And one might write tiny letters, yet have very wide spaces, and this would then show generosity. However, there are variations even in these general rules, which will be discussed here.

In order to be able to judge spacing between lines of handwriting, it is essential for the graphologist to have writing done on paper which has no printed lines. In children's handwritings it is often hard to judge distance between lines, as for the first few years in school they are made to write on lined paper. Also, it might be hard to measure spaces on a postcard, as the writer usually has to tighten up the writing and spaces to fit the message into a cramped space.

In the preceding chapter we discussed a person's attitude toward money, as shown in the width or narrowness of the margins. Here we show an additional way (the spacings) to further bear out what may be seen in the margins.

When you first look at a sheet of handwriting, before you start to analyze its details, you are aware of the arrangement of the complete sheet. If the lines and words have evenly-spaced distances between them, you can surmise the person has a sense of order. But if the distances between words and lines are irregular, the indication is that the writer has a rather disorganized way of thought and action.

Also, good taste may be seen in the placement of the writing on the whole page, just as you can quickly evaluate a person's taste by the way he or she is dressed (either neatly or in a disheveled manner).

Generally, wide spaces between lines and words mean a generous spirit, a broadness of attitude. However, there are variations in the size and shape of letter formations which may either detract or add to this general definition.

SPACING BETWEEN LINES

1. In this illustration you see large letter formations but little or no spacing between the words and the lines of writing. The large writing shows one who likes to meet people (in Chapter XIII the size of writing is fully discussed). Thus this person may give the impression of being a free spender because of his expansive manner. Yet, the lack of spacing shows the writer does not spend generously, even though one might think he does.

2. This writing shows the same size letters, but the distance between the words and lines is large. Here then

we see the desire not only to spend for one's own pleasure but to be generous to others as well.

1. going my way
here it is

2. going my
here it

This same principle applies to writing which is done with small letters. The one who writes small is usually reserved, so one may not know just how he thinks or spends, and the impression may be gained that he is thrifty. Yet, if the small handwriting shows very wide spaces between words and lines of writing, that person has a generous spirit. But if the tiny handwriting has very narrow or no spaces, then it is a sign of frugality toward oneself and toward others, plus a good deal of caution.

SPACING BETWEEN WORDS

Usually the spacing between words follows the same general pattern of distance between lines. However, there are some cases where the spaces are wide between words but narrow between lines of writing; or, in reverse, narrow between words but wide between lines.

1. Wide or narrow space

2. Wide or narrow

1. If the writing contains narrow, squeezed letters, with narrow spaces between the words, it indicates a person who is overly cautious and may become too interested in things and details, rather than have an interest in people and ideas.

2. The same narrow words, when widely spaced apart, show the writer has the same critical and cautious attitude in appraising things and details, but he also has a more broad-minded attitude in understanding people.

IRREGULARITY OF SPACES

When the spaces between words and lines of writing are done in an uneven, irregular manner, this condition is not analyzed separately. It has to be studied in correlation to the many other signs in the handwriting which may produce the basic cause for such a lack of organization.

DISCONNECTED LETTERS

In a cursive handwriting you may sometimes find the writer makes breaks in the connecting strokes between letters in a word.

1. dis connected words

2. connected words

1. This is a sign of intuition; the writer may rely to great extent on a hunch and on his spontaneous response to people and ideas and places.

2. When there are no breaks in the letters, the person uses more practical thinking methods than relying on hunches. The mind works in a logical manner, leaving as little to chance as is necessary.

You may see a sample of handwriting where some words are connected, and in other words there are breaks between the letters. In such a case the writer possesses both logic and intuition, and the analyst has to determine which is the more dominant trait. If there are only 10 per cent of the words connected and 90 per cent disconnected, then it is indicated that the person can (in extreme necessity) work things out through logical reasoning; however, the impulse is to rely on intuition. But, in reverse, if the handwriting specimen shows only 15 per cent of the words disconnected, and 85 per cent connected, the analyst knows that the writer has some intuition which may enable him to get a quicker head-start on some ideas, but he does not rely on a hunch and actually (when the plan needs to be tackled) he becomes practical in his reasoning.

When we get these combinations of disconnected and connected words in one sample of writing, it usually shows the person to be versatile in ideas and tastes and abilities, rather than to be in a fixed pattern of thought or action. Of course, this has to be borne out by correlation to other signs in the writing.

Sometimes it is baffling to a graphologist to be able to discern whether the breaks in the letters in a word are natural ones, or whether they are part of the manuscript (block printing) method of penmanship. Those who are taught Palmer or other cursive methods of writing are naturally taught to connect each letter in a word; but when the child matures and starts to write naturally (not in the forced manner taught by the penmanship teacher), he may start to disconnect some of the letters in cursive writing. This, of course, shows a natural tendency to intuition. However, a child or an adult who still uses the manuscript method of writing is not necessarily making the breaks between letters in a word because of intuition (but may be making those disconnections only because he was so taught in that block printing method of penmanship). The graphologist must be circumspect when analyzing such a style of writing.

Also, people who print in their work (such as architects, draftsmen, engineers, etc.) naturally disconnect the letters in a word (because that is how printing is written). So here, too, the handwriting analyst must use care in determining whether that specimen shows intuition or whether the breaks in the letters of the words are just the "tools of the trade" in the printing used by that person in his special work.

CHAPTER ELEVEN

Pressure of Pen or Pencil

When the first studies of pressure were made, there was not the diversity of writing instruments which are now on the market. So, when the pioneers in the field of handwriting analysis made their findings on the meanings of heavy or light pressure, they were not stymied by the variations of pens or pencils now in use.

For instance, if a person writes with a ball-point pen, the writing is light; when the ink cartridge in the ball point pen starts to peter out, the pen starts to sputter and leaves smudges in the writing. Thus, the graphologist cannot know if the person naturally writes with a light or a heavy pressure.

A pencil which is of the propel-and-repel refill type usually has an inserted lead of hard substance; so it is not possible to know whether the user naturally would write with a light or heavy pressure.

The most recent style of pen is the one with a point made of a fiber (usually nylon), which in principle represents the original "brush pen" used by the ancient Chinese. These new pens with the fiber nibs are free-flowing and produce heavy lines; thus the handwriting analyst cannot discern the natural pressure here either.

While most graphologists contend that it is not possible to see natural pressure when writing is done with a pencil, but insist on seeing a specimen of handwriting done with a pen (the standard fountain pen or the pen-holder with a steel nib), I have made experiments with pencil-writing and find that it is just as easy to see differences in pressure as with a standard type of pen. The pencil should not be of the propelling type heretofore mentioned, but should be the usual wooden pencil with the usual graphite lead.

In many instances I opened a brand new box of a dozen pencils, with a #2 lead (which is neither too hard nor too soft), and handed a pencil to each of twelve people and told them to write a few lines and sign their names. I did not dictate to them, as that would not produce as spontaneous a writing as if they were left to their own choice of what to write. Every time I tried this experiment, I found that each person produced a different pressure from the other; there were all degrees of pressure from very light to very heavy. So that writing with a pencil does not hide the natural pressure any more than a standard pen does.

On the market are also new types of pencils, generally termed "china markers," which are of crayon consistency, and they can write on glazed surfaces. Handwriting with such a pencil is definitely not a good sample for purposes of determining pressure, as that pencil always produces a heavy line.

The graphologist must also exercize care (in analyzing pressure) when the sample consists of a photocopy of the handwriting or is a reprint of the writing in a newspaper. The thickness of a handwriting stroke may often be exaggerated, or the lines broken and jagged, when the writing is photographed.

The foregoing all shows that when judging the thickness or thinness of strokes of handwriting, the graphologist must be very cautious and should ask (if he or she is not too sure) what type of pen or pencil was used in the specimen of handwriting. It is sometimes necessary for the graphologist to pass over the pressure factor and make the analysis from all the other signs which are seen in the handwriting.

A usual question posed to the handwriting analyst by a client is, "What kind of pen (or pencil) should I use?" and there is no answer to that. The person who uses the pen or pencil is the only one who can know what is best, by practicing with a few writing instruments until the most comfortable one is acceptable. It is like telling a person what shoes or gloves to wear in order to feel comfortable; only the wearer of those articles of apparel can know by actually testing them for proper ease and fit. Generally, a person whose traits would be reflected in a heavy pressure will choose a heavy pen point and a soft pencil; the one whose personality traits would be reflected in a light-pressure handwriting will usually select a pen with a thin point and a pencil with a hard lead.

TESTING GENUINE PRESSURE

Sometimes a writing which is written with heavy lines may not be a genuine pressure; it may be the result of a pen with a heavy point. And some writing may appear to have a very light pressure; this may be due to a pen with a thin point. So the actual way to test the pressure, to know if it is only the result of the size of pen point used or is actually a genuine pressure, is for the handwriting analyst to run the tips of the fingers over the writing *on the reverse side of the sheet of paper!* The sensitive finger tips will be able to feel the indentation (tiny ridges) made by the writer who bore down with the pen (even if the pressure looks light), or they will be able to tell if there is no indentation at all (showing no real, genuine pressure even though the writing looks heavy in pressure).

SIGNIFICANCE OF PRESSURE

Pressure in handwriting is divided into heavy, medium, and light for easy purposes of studying its meaning when making an analysis. Some handwritings show variable pressures. Just because a dozen people may all write with heavy or light or medium pressure, it does not mean that these twelve people all have the same personality only because of similar pressure; their handwritings must be studied in all other areas, and some may contradict others, as far as personality traits are disclosed.

Generally, pressure of the pen indicates an expression of the vitality and energy of the person, or the lack of these traits.

HEAVY PRESSURE

When the person writes with heavy pressure, it signifies he is an extrovert, has a strong desire for material gratification, and has an aggressiveness which is not easily discouraged.

1. If the heavy strokes appear in a handwriting which is done with rather commonplace formations, the person is interested in his material acquisitions and comforts and has strong physical appetites.

2. The heavy pressure which appears in a writing where there are some original letter formations will also show vitality and desire for material and physical satisfaction; but, in addition, these interesting formations show good taste, a desire to be in surroundings of beauty, and the instincts are usually on a much higher plane than shown in the writing in Item 1.

1. Heavy pressure

2. This gives you

When the pressure of the pen is heavier on the horizontal strokes (such as the crossing bar of the "t" and the connecting strokes between the letters in a word, or the top of the letter "r" (rather than on its two vertical strokes), we find a writer who has will power, who wants to live on an expensive scale. These heavy horizontal strokes also show a person who has a vital personality and does not like too much solitude, either in social life or in the work which that person may pursue. The writer may be domineering when placed in a leadership position.

In a reverse situation, where the heavy pressure is more pronounced on the vertical strokes, such as the downward stroke of the letters "h" and "l" and "t" and on the lower letters "y" and "g," we find the writer has all the desires of the person whose heavy pressure is done on horizontal strokes (as told in the preceding paragraph). Yet, this person is usually inhibited, and the yearnings for power and material things are secretive and not expressed. This writer may not have the inner power to carry out the desires, although he may have a defiant outer manner.

While heavy pressure discloses extroversion and aggressiveness, the person may not always succeed in a job or profession toward which he aims if he becomes too aggressive and if he is overly ambitious for the quick result.

And some heavy-pressure writers have to adapt to a situation where they must function in a subordinate role; while this is contrary to the basic nature of the person, he or she might be able to do well in that situation if it is necessary to do so. So even the person with the heaviest pressure of writing might adapt to a mild and meek way of life, and perhaps even enjoy it.

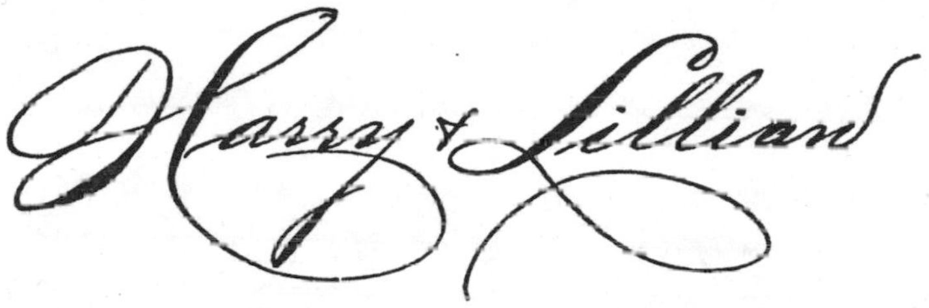

This illustration is not a genuine sample of heavy pressure on a vertical (downward) stroke, as it shows a highly stylized manner of writing which follows the charming Spencerian method which was fashionable in the late nineteenth century. The person who writes this way is conventional and has a respect for tradition and a desire for gracious living. The novice graphologist must guard against mistaking this lovely, old-fashioned penmanship for a true heavy-pressure writing.

LIGHT PRESSURE

The general graphological rules covering light pressure say the person has idealistic aspirations and is not motivated by the materialistic urges which are seen in writing of heavy pressure. Also, the introvert usually writes with light pressure. Yet, not all people who press lightly on their pens or pencils are completely similar, and there are variations one must recognize and study when making an analysis.

1. plain writing

2. I made my mark!

3. where is Manhattan?

1. When light-pressure writing contains soft, rounded formations, the writer is unselfish and has tender feelings. There is no aggressiveness or desire for personal aggrandizement in this handwriting.

2. If the writing contains original formations it has the tender qualities of the foregoing writer; but, in addition, we find more individuality in the imagination and high aspirations of an idealistic nature.

3. If the forms are sometimes indefinite and the base line is unsteady, this shows a hesitancy to go ahead with new ideas, and not enough self-confidence to proceed with a definite purpose in life or to accept responsibilities.

In spite of these gentle qualities which are the basis of light-pressure writing, many people who write this way are able to function in their personal and business lives as leaders, when they possess originality and intelligence and resourcefulness, and when they are faced with a strong incentive. So it is possible for these sensitive people to "step out of character" when the motive is sufficiently strong. This is expressed here, because many student graphologists may stop in wonderment when they are told that someone with a very light pressure handwriting is doing a fine executive or leadership job. This is just a reminder that the handwriting does not tell only what a person may do on the surface, but what the inner person really is.

MEDIUM PRESSURE

This is the writing between heavy and light, so that the person is neither too aggressive, extroverted, and materialistic, nor too idealistic, sensitive, and introverted. This person might be called the ambivert. The analysis, therefore, has to be done more on the other signs in the handwriting rather than on the medium pressure by itself.

MUDDY HANDWRITING

When a writer does not use the same pressure throughout his handwriting; when he varies the thickness of the strokes, and you actually feel that it was "written with a pen dipped in mud" rather than with flowing ink, you find a personality that is jealous, self-indulgent, has no sensitivity, lacks refinement, and may balk at having to cooperate with others unless he feels there is some advantage which will accrue to himself.

The muddy writing shows a good deal of physical vitality, and the person is motivated by material ambition (even though he may talk a good line of "idealism").

UNEVEN PRESSURE

You may examine a handwriting which varies in pressure, with some of the formations written in light or medium or heavy pressure, and you find an inconsistent person who is easily swayed by his fluctuating moods. This writer is usually very sensitive and goes through a good deal of indecision. This is usually an irritable person, and in some cases he may display quick temper.

If such pressure changes occur in a young person's handwriting, it may be that full, mature development has not yet occurred. But an adult who varies the pressure usually shows the sensitive and irritable traits which are part of an indecisive nature.

The signature is not always written with the same pressure as the rest of the handwriting, which has an interesting graphological significance. This is discussed in Chapter XIX on Signatures.

DOES AGE SHOW IN PRESSURE?

An erroneous conception is that children write with heavy pressure and that old people therefore write with light pressure. The assumption is that children are so vital and robust and older people are feeble. Nothing could be more to the contrary!

A vital, extroverted child may write with a heavy pressure; whereas his introverted, sensitive sibling may write with a light pressure. And his grandparents may be energetic, lively-spirited people who write with heavy formations; or his friend's older relatives may be gentle, sensitive, introverted people who write with a light pressure of the pen.

The age of the person does not necessarily relegate him or her to any one kind of attitude or energy or ability. So the pressure of the pen or pencil in no way relates to the chronological age.

CHAPTER TWELVE

Legible or Illegible Writing

Judging the personality merely because the handwriting is legible and "good-looking" (or reversely, because the writing is illegible and "bad-looking") is as unfair as saying, "This person has a beautiful character because she has a beautiful face," or "He must have a terrible personality because he has ugly facial features." Legibility or illegibility is actually the "face" of the handwriting, and in itself it does not portray the whole inner person. This sign in a handwriting needs to be carefully studied in correlation with the other features of the writing.

The teacher naturally strives to make each child write "the perfect hand," and it may not be within the innate traits of that child to be able to follow a strict penmanship method; he or she may find it a laborious process, especially if the child does not have any manual dexterity. Therefore, in analyzing a handwriting for its signs of legibility or illegibility, the graphologist should take into consideration whether the specimen was written by a very young person (who may still be in a stage of intellectual development and whose handwriting may change its form later on) or by an adult whose writing is already set in its pattern.

Not all legible handwriting means the same, as this sign has many variations.

1. Here is careful, legible writing; the formations do not contain any letters that are particularly original or distinctive. It is an average style of cursive penmanship. This reveals a careful thinker and worker who is cooperative in spirit, one who may enjoy being in touch with new ideas yet is basically conventional. This careful, legible handwriting also shows a hesitancy to embark on altogether new paths of endeavor, before the person is convinced that it is wise to do so. Usually we find this writer to be consistent and not apt to take uncalculated risks.

2. When the legible writing is small, it discloses a person who likes to do work which requires application to minute details, and to produce meticulous results. This writer shows patience in dealing with facts and figures, and has an admiration for things of finest workmanship. Socially this person does not need a widespread circle of friends; this one may be more at ease with a small group of people with whom he or she can share common interests. Generally this small, legible writing belongs to a person who has received training along some specific line of work and who does not rush ahead into new directions without first studying each detail of the new steps to be taken. This writer does not take things for granted.

3. Legible writing which shows printed as well as cursive forms portrays the person whose mind is constructively imaginative. Original ideas are part of this writer's thinking, but they are not merely daydreams and the ideas

I hope this will in

1. further your cause

~~money order for your services~~

2. ~~receive the analysis shortly,~~

in the late autumn

in a hollow at the

3. and I in boots

analysis and

be delighted to

4. your remarks.

However they were

pleasantry and I

anxious to hear those

5. my personality that

are usually put to practical use. The clear thinking is shown in the legibility, and the ability to use the mind in a resourceful and constructive manner is borne out in the printed letters.

4. This handwriting, while legible, is rather stilted and it shows that the writer consciously strives to acquire an "elegant hand" which will place him or her on a higher plane than others. However, the trained graphologist sees that the rhythm of the writing is not a free one; the writer pulls back and hesitates while making each formation (to create an "impressive hand"); this then is a reflection of the cautious and self-conscious manner in which this person thinks. It is not spontaneous handwriting, and shows the writer is hesitant to take chances.

5. A writing which seems to be illegible and hard to decipher at first glance may not be hard to read once the handwriting analyst gives it full study and sort of de-codes the unusual letter formations which the writer has devised. Louise Rice, in her book *Character Reading from Handwriting,* called this the "legible-cryptic" style of writing. The writer is independent in thinking, and some of his or her ideas are unusual and inventive. It is not easy to understand this person, because there is an aloofness in manner (which may be covering up an innate shyness, and other signs in the handwriting may bear this out). Individuality in taste is also seen in this style of writing. If you cannot decipher this legible-cryptic illustration (which was cut from a full-page letter, so some of these words are not complete and the sentence may not make sense), here is the way it reads: "However, they were . . . plimentary and I . . . anxious to hear these . . . my personality that . . ."

LEGIBILITY IF ENGLISH IS SECOND LANGUAGE

An interesting development in recent years is writing done in the English language by people who, in adult life, learned it as their second language. In a handwriting analysis project I conducted for a period of over ten years, for a business organization, I received hundreds of handwritings from people in Hawaii and the Philippine Islands. In most cases their original language and handwritings had been Chinese, Japanese, or Spanish. Also hundreds of writing specimens were received from people in the Latin American countries, whose original handwritings had been in Spanish or Portuguese.

In 99 per cent of the cases their English formations were legible, in a stilted manner; they used copy-book formations in the way the child is first taught how to write. Their handwritings in English were the result of craftsmanship in copying the letter forms rather than in free-flowing handwritings. Therefore, these specimens of writing were not spontaneous expressions of their personality traits, and analyses should be made from the original language they were taught as children.

The children born in those countries, who are taught English (as well as whatever other language they use), do not write in the "manufactured" way the adults do. They write the freer "American style" handwriting, and of course their specimens of writing lend themselves to analysis.

To offset the foregoing, there are people in all countries who are not native Americans or British and who learn to write the English language as adults. They do not write in a mechanical manner; their handwritings are spontaneous, in no matter what language they write, and they are truly internationally-minded people who can adapt to any country in which they choose to live. And their handwritings are legible or illegible and are analyzed accordingly.

ILLEGIBILITY

Before the handwriting analyst proceeds to examine the writing on its sign of illegibility, it is necessary first to analyze all the other signs in the writing to find out the cause for the resultant illegibility. It is difficult for the graphologist to quickly see the significance of illegibility, and much care must be taken in its study.

There are many degrees of illegibility; some handwritings in this category may be written in such a confused manner, with some of the letter forms entirely missing and some completely unidentifiable, and some illegible writing having many disorderly formations included, that the only conclusion the handwriting analyst can reach is that this person is either uneducated, or has a totally disorganized mental attitude, or is irritable and cannot stick to a routine, or has complete disregard for his fellow human beings so that he doesn't bother to make himself clear in other ways (not just his handwriting). However, this conclusion must not be reached as a result of a snap judgment, and all the other signs must be carefully studied before a true result can be achieved by the graphologist.

In this illustrated specimen we find a different kind of illegibility, and this contains some positive traits which offset some of the negative ones. The illegibility here is produced by a quick mind; this person cannot relax, cannot concentrate on details, doesn't want to be a conformist and stick to routine, and generally he is impatient for results. He is such a speedy thinker and worker that he hasn't the time to devote to writing legibly (any more than he thinks or acts "legibly" in all areas of his life). In this specimen we find original adult formations, and not the immature copy-book style of formations. This writer is trying to eliminate as many writing strokes as possible, yet he may crowd his mind and his life with a lot of nonessentials even though he is trying to rid himself of them. When a person writes this way, he or she does not want to be told or shown a thing more than once; the reactions are spontaneous, though they may not always show good judgment. While this writer has many commendable traits, he may not reap the benefits of them because of his lack of organization of mind and action. Such a personality, because it is a puzzlement, may be most attractive and intriguing to others.

SPECIAL CASES OF ILLEGIBILITY

If a person has written in a legible manner for years and years, and suddenly the handwriting becomes illegible, it may signify an illness which affects the muscles and nerves, or it may be due to some mental confusion, or some other contributing cause which is beyond the control of the writer. Of course this may be temporary, and the writing may again become legible. However, if the graphologist comes across such a case, the wise procedure is to refuse to analyze the handwriting for the client and leave any diagnosis to a physician.

Some people who become permanently disabled and cannot coordinate the mind and muscles and nerves, may often produce handwriting which is completely illegible and is just a scrawl of disorganized lines. And, as the disability progresses, the confusion of the writing may also progress. But this is also a case to be handled by the medical profession. Of course these cases are worthy of the graphologist's clinical study, but should not be discussed with a layman in a graphologist–client relationship.

We have already mentioned the illegibility of the doctor's prescription blank, in Chapter VI, to which kindly refer.

You may come across a specimen of writing where the words start out legibly, and toward the end of the word there are no more letter formations but just a straight or wavy line slithers along the sheet. This is not truly an illegible way of writing, and such formation is discussed at the end of the following chapter which tells about size of words and letters.

CHAPTER THIRTEEN

Size of Writing

Handwriting size is generally either small or medium or large. The "medium" is the average size of writing taught in school, and is considered as the norm from which we regard a handwriting either as small or large. Some people may write in various sizes of handwriting, dependent on the sheet of paper and the condition under which the writing takes place.

For example, a writer who naturally makes large formations may produce a very small handwriting within a prescribed space of a postcard, or when writing on a narrow sheet in an address book, or when having to fill out certain forms. Also, the one who writes large may be using a sheet which has printed lines on it, and he may therefore write smaller in order not to have the writing go above or below the printed base line.

Or, a person who naturally writes with very small formations may sometimes write larger when wanting to produce a certain effect (such as in a party invitation or on a greeting card, etc.).

If a person says, "I make different sizes of letters," it behooves the graphologist to ask to see various samples of that person's writing and to ask that writer which is his or her natural size of writing. When such information is not available, the professional handwriting analyst is usually able to know (through study of other signs in the writing) which size is natural for that person.

If a photocopy or a newspaper reprint of a handwriting is submitted for analysis, the graphologist should ascertain if this is the actual size of the writing, because in many instances the handwriting might be reduced or enlarged in the process of its being reproduced.

Whether the child was taught to write with small, medium, or large letter forms, when he is an adult this will make no difference in the eventual size of the writing he produces. Some children taught to write large may, in mature development of the mind, write much smaller in adult life. But others who may have learned to write with small formations may, upon maturing, write with medium or large letter forms later on. Some child may have an eye defect or simple myopia, and when learning penmanship may see the letter formations smaller or larger than they really are, and may copy the letters in that size. But, on being given corrective eyeglasses, the size of the writing may change as the child reads the letters in their actual size. Of course, some people never change their size of writing from the day they got their first penmanship lesson to their days of maturity.

SMALL SIZE

Generally, a small writing signifies a mind that is able to concentrate on details, facts, and figures; the person usually produces meticulous work in whatever field he or she is. The manner is usually not an aggressive one, even though that person may possess much determination. Enthusiasms are generally held in check.

Small writing which is done clearly and which contains capital letters that are proportionate in size (not too large) is indicative of a person who does not have any pretenses.

If the capital letters are too tiny (in relation to the size of the small letters), the person is not sufficiently self-confident and hesitates to assert himself. Sometimes the modesty is carried too far and keeps this writer from going after things which he might be able to do.

But, if the small writing contains proportionately large capitals, it is an interesting sign that while the writer is reserved and cautious, he has developed a more dominant attitude than is natural for him; also he has pride.

When the small handwriting shows original and distinctive formations, and the capital letters are graceful and artistic, we find that while this person innately does meticulous thinking and working, in addition he has been able to consciously develop a more outgoing personality and may be more courageous in showing enthusiasm and expressing ideas.

Small handwriting may sometimes go to the extreme of being too tiny, and the spaces between the letters in a word and between words are tightly squeezed together, so that it is hard to read (and sometimes a magnifying glass needs to be used). This person may have some fine mental qualities and be able to study minute facts and concentrate on detailed work; yet the exceedingly squeezed writing may show he is not capable of fulfilling all his ideas and abilities. This writer may be affectionate and desirous of sharing his or her life with others; yet sometimes he may be misjudged by those who mistake the reserve for lack of friendliness.

LARGE SIZE

In general, a large handwriting shows a person to be expansive, one who does not want to be tied down to any work or personal matters if it would mean having to be alone too much of the time. Other signs in the handwriting might show this writer has the capacity for concentration and logical reasoning, but no work or profession would really suit him unless the human element were the most important factor in connection with such work. The personality is usually an outgoing one, and this writer likes an interesting social-life atmosphere in his work, his home, and his hobbies.

Large handwriting which has graceful and artistically made capital letters, and which just seems to flow across the page, reveals a personality that is usually gregarious, romantic, and who enjoys lively interchange of conversation and may sometimes be "the life of the party." Such a writer likes to be noticed, to be admired, and he may be conceited but it's usually not a neurotic trait and is a sign of a robust attitude toward life.

When the aforementioned large, graceful handwriting achieves a size that is exceedingly large, it signifies a sense of grandeur. This person may think of himself almost as if he were "royalty," and he likes to receive acclaim and adulation from others.

If the large writing includes capitals that are small in proportion to the size of the small letters, the neophyte graphologist may not be able to comprehend the situation.

However, this is really simple, because it shows that while the aggressive manner (the large writing) is put on to impress others, the small capital letters reveal the inner personality to be much less self-confident than the outer manner displays.

Large writing which is narrow and squeezed together (often this has angular formations rather than free-flowing rounded ones) indicates a person of great determination. The largeness of the writing may show a desire for recognition and approbation, or if very large, a sense of grandeur. But the narrowness offsets any outgoing qualities by showing that the personality is not a compromising one, that the sense of justice may be inflexible, and that there is a critical attitude in accepting anyone as a close friend. So this kind of large writing cannot be put into the same category as the others mentioned heretofore, and has to be studied and analyzed with much care in order to see why such a large handwriting can possess such contradictory traits.

MEDIUM SIZE

Not much can be said which applies exclusively to the medium size of writing. It is the "happy medium" between the small and the large handwriting, and the personality is usually easy to understand.

The person who writes with medium size generally strikes a good balance between the head and the heart, is not too reserved nor too outgoing, and can usually find some way of adapting to situations or people without creating any fuss about it.

Medium size of writing is not too important a factor in

handwriting analysis, but it is studied in correlation with the other factors in the writing.

VARIATIONS IN SIZE

In a small handwriting, when the letters show many variations in the size, this signifies the writer has fluctuating moods and may also be sensitive.

In large writing, when the letters vary in size, the indication here too is that the person has variable moods and is sensitive. However, the one who writes large will show these moods on the surface more than the one who writes with small formations.

A letter may be written wide at the top but is made narrower at the bottom, as for instance the letter "o" would be more rounded and wider at the top and less rounded at the bottom. This reveals a person who is hesitant to tell too much to another and is usually very cautious.

But the letter which is narrower at the top but becomes wider at the bottom shows a person who is the reverse of the former. This writer is inclined to confide more in others, and perhaps at times he is not sufficiently discreet in doing so.

TAPERING WRITING

A word (or a line, or a whole sheet) of handwriting may change its size; the writer does this unconsciously rather than intentionally.

1. When the writing starts with a large formation, then tapers down in size until the end is smaller, this discloses the person who may start out to tell everything, but he is

really discreet so he catches himself in time and ends up telling as little as he thinks the other person should know. This may be found in the handwritings of people who are fluent conversationalists. It is easy to picture a wide open mouth (the beginning of the word) which then shuts itself tightly down (the end of the word) as this person regains control of his talking process.

1. writing

2. writing

3. writing

2. But here we see the opposite; the word (or a line, or a whole sheet) starts out with small formations, but it gets larger and at the end it is much bigger than at the beginning of the writing. This person tries to keep a secret but just cannot help telling all despite the best intentions not to divulge too much. Here the mouth may be kept shut at first, but it gets bigger and opens wide (and so the handwriting betrays that personality trait).

3. And now we come to the diplomat. When we see this trailing off at the end of a word, we find the person who can speak most interestingly for hours but really tells very little or nothing. Aside from being secretive, as the formation shown in Item 1, this person is also a diplomat and is usually shrewd in knowing how to deal with people.

CHAPTER FOURTEEN

Capital Letters

The capital letters are usually written in proportion to the size of the lowercase (the small) letters. However, sometimes the capitals are too small or too large (reference was made to this in the preceding chapter), and sometimes they are simple or they are ornamented. Thus, the capital letter in itself is an interesting sign in some handwritings when it stands out conspicuously from the rest of the writing.

SIZE OF CAPITALS

When the child learns to write, the capital letters are usually large, so that is not to be taken for too much significance. But when an adult makes capitals which are noticeably larger than the small letters, it reveals a desire to be noticed by others. When analyzed in conjunction with other signs in the writing, the graphologist may find this large capital to indicate pride or desire for achievement, or perhaps vanity. But, whatever other signs show, the large capital in itself means that the writer is not the shrinking, modest personality. The one who makes the large capitals in an ornamental style may also be seeking to achieve social prestige.

The capital letter which is small in proportion to the lowercase letters is, therefore, the reverse of the foregoing one. This writer has a modest personality and does not try to take the center of the stage and be in the limelight (as the person with the large capitals is prone to do). And if the writer makes the capital letters too small in proportion to the rest of the writing, it may show modesty to a fault; it is also perhaps a sign of being too self-conscious.

When the capitals are not different from the rest of the writing in size or style of penmanship (not too large, not too small, not overornamented), the graphologist does not need to spend time in studying the capital letters by themselves, but just analyzes them as a part of the entire specimen of handwriting.

CAPITALS IN LOWERCASE

Occasionally a signature is made without any capital letters, or even the whole page of writing does not have capitals:

did you see john? he
came to new york last
august.

Here the handwriting analyst has to be very cautious, and in examining the other signs in the writing he will need to determine whether the person is overly modest and thus makes no capitals at all; or if the writer is merely following a fad (often prevalent among college students) in emulating the style of "no capital letters," which was used by the writer *e. e. cummings*. Or, the one who uses no capitals may be trying to be different from the crowd and very sophisticated, and is thus asserting his or her own ego by defying the accepted form of capitalizing names and beginnings of sentences.

However, if the handwriting does not show any other signs that reveal such individualistic (or striving to be nonconformist) attitudes, it may be that the writer is not sufficiently schooled to know that capital letters must be used, and that he makes all lowercase letters due to lack of basic education.

It behooves the graphologist to use much care when a "no capitals" handwriting appears, and not make a snap judgment.

PRINTED CAPITALS

A printed or semiprinted capital may be found in a handwriting that is otherwise composed of cursive formations.

The Merry month of
May. Happy Days.

This person has a constructive mind and is usually able to think and work in a resourceful manner and tries to find shortcut methods. The mind prefers to rid itself of nonessentials and get down to basics.

The printed form of capitals in a cursive handwriting is done unconsciously, and I am often asked by my clients (who will notice their printed or semiprinted forms) why this should happen, as they usually think it is a sign of carelessness on their part. When I tell them that these printed capitals show they have grown up and are using their abilities in a constructive manner, they feel quite relieved.

Simple, printed capitals are also a sign of good taste; these people rarely like anything that is cluttered in design or workmanship.

Of course, the foregoing explanation of printed capital letters may not apply to the person who deliberately (consciously) sets out to make printed capitals. The graphologist can usually discern this, as the printed letters look forced and they do not have a natural rhythm of writing.

ORNAMENTED CAPITALS

The more elaborate the capital letter, the more the person wants to be noticed.

1. A M L

2. A

1. These writers need to have an active social life; they may join organizations so they may be part of busy groups, and in their jobs they want to work where there are many people around them. Why? Because they want to be noticed, and if they are alone too much, there will be no one to pay attention to them. They usually make charming hostesses and gracious hosts. Their tastes are often flamboyant.

2. This lovely old-fashioned capital letter is known as "the protective A", and it reveals a desire to protect those who are weak and poor, to be of help wherever possible in making other people happy, with no thought of selfish gain. These protective people are often led by their sympathetic hearts and not by practical thought when it comes to helping others. An interesting point here is that we find this protective "A" in the handwriting of Abraham Lincoln. And Amelia Earheart, the aviatrix who was lost in flight, also made this "A," and she was a social worker before she took up aviation.

CAPITAL "M" AND "N"

Generally these capital letters are analyzed in the same manner as explained in the foregoing about size, whether printed or ornamented. But the "M" (and the "N") often takes on special significance.

1. When the letter starts with an incurve, in an angular form, it shows clannishness though not very cooperative. The writer is critical and may often be stubborn about minor details.

2. This rounded incurve also reveals a clannish instinct, with a spirit of cooperation. This person is usually conventional in attitudes and activities.

3. An outward curve at the beginning of the letter is a sign of a gregarious person. This writer may sometimes like to break away from convention; however, he does respect tradition and may exercise caution when a decision must be made to take a new step forward.

4. When the first loop (or point, or arcade) of the capital is taller than the other two loops (or the one other loop in the "N"), it shows a person who has a fighting pride, will not admit defeat too soon, and keeps forging ahead in a desire to achieve personal success. This writer does not want to be in a subordinate position, whether in work or in personal relationships.

5. When the last loop in the capital is higher than the others, the writer is apt to create an impression of being more retiring than he or she really is. That tall last loop in the letter is a giveaway of a person who is stubborn and self-assertive, and may be most tenacious in going after a desired result. As the outer and the inner personality may not always match, this person is usually hard to understand, and the graphologist may have to look to the other signs in the writing to find out what this person is really like.

6. In the "M" where the middle loop is tallest, the

personality may often be a puzzlement to others. This writer may have unusual ideas of his own, though he may not readily share them with other people. He is usually concerned with his own self and is not too outgoing toward others.

VARIATIONS IN CAPITALS

Some people may make a capital letter in different styles. By itself, such a variation does not have one meaning; but the graphologist must see how the capital letters relate to the other signs in the handwriting, and then must determine if the different styles of one capital are due to lack of concentration, versatility, inconsistency, or whatever traits are seen in the entire specimen of the writing.

CAPITAL "I" REVEALS PRIDE, EGO

The "I" is a complete word in itself; it is a first person pronoun; it reflects the ego of the writer.

The formation of the letter may be regarded in the same way as all other capitals, as to size, simplicity of printing, or elaboration of ornamentation. However, the capital "I" in itself has further meaning.

1. The "I" which is done simply and in proportion to the size of the small letters shows a person who likes to cooperate with others. There is no pretense in this personality.

2. When the "I" is inflated in size (and accompanied by other large capitals), the writer has personal vanity and likes to be noticed and applauded for every achievement, large or small. Also, this is a sign of a sociable person, one

who needs companionship in personal life as well as in work. But if the inflated "I" is the only large capital letter, and the other capitals are simple and in proportion to the size of writing, the handwriting analyst deduces that the

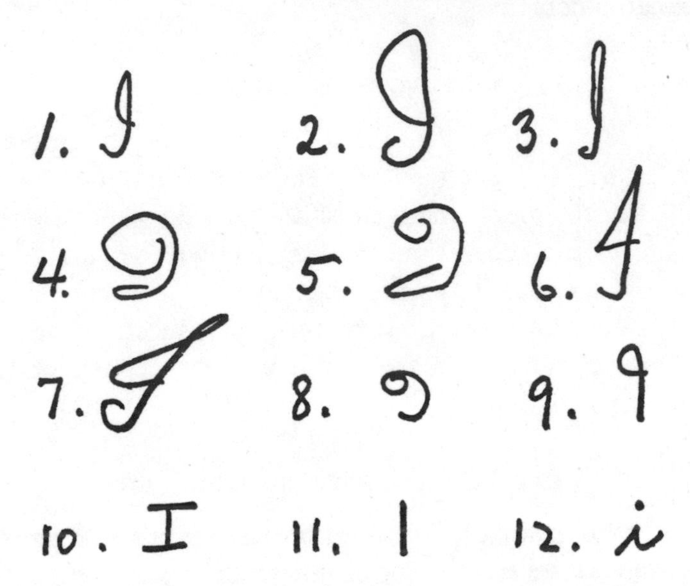

vanity is only a surface trait (a sort of "show-off" attitude put on by the writer to delude himself about his ego), but the vanity is really not deep-seated.

3. When the "I" is tall and narrow, it discloses a person who does not possess vanity, but who does have much pride of the clan. This writer is loyal to home and family ties and does not make a bid for attention.

4. When the "I" looks almost like a fat capital "Q," it reveals a person of conventional attitudes. This writer desires social activities and is a congenial companion. There may be a little vanity, but it is more in fun than an actual conceited trait.

5. The letter with a little bulb on top and a rather wide, squat bottom is usually made taller than the other letters. This means the same as the "I" in foregoing Item 4.

6. When the "I" is made with angular formations, it reveals a critical mind. This writer does not want to waste time but prefers to aim directly toward a goal which will result from a definite purpose.

7. This is rather an old-fashioned "I" which usually portrays a reserved manner and tact in getting along with others. This writer does not rush ahead on impulse but prefers to carefully consider all new moves.

8. If the "I" is pulled backward in an otherwise forward-leaning handwriting, it shows the person is hesitant to take an aggressive step ahead and will generally be cautious before coming to any new decision. Sometimes this also shows lack of sufficient self-confidence, especially if the pulled-back "I" should be too small in proportion to the size of the handwriting.

9. This simple letter shows the writer has pride but is not egotistical. The mind exercizes control over the emotions, and the tastes are good and unpretentious.

10. When the "I" resembles the Roman numeral "I," and appears in an otherwise cursive writing, it indicates the person is confident of his ideas and abilities, is generally able to keep a cool attitude, and takes pride in accomplishment. This writer generally has many constructive ideas, and if the rest of the writing bears this out, he or she may possibly use the ideas in a resourceful manner to produce interesting results.

11. This plain, unadulterated line which portrays the "I" may possess many of the qualities which the foregoing "I" in Item 10 has. However, this writer may have more

reserve and is interested in things and people of intellectual stature.

12. When the lowercase "i" is used, it may be lack of education or perhaps faddish sophistication. Kindly see the explanation given earlier in this chapter in the section captioned "CAPITALS IN LOWERCASE."

VARIATIONS IN CAPITAL "I"

A sample of handwriting may contain many different versions of the capital "I" form. In such a case the writer may be versatile and imaginative (which would need to be verified in other signs in the handwriting), and it shows that the person takes himself with a sense of humor and is usually flexible in changing situations. When a person makes variations of the capital "I" (which is the representation of the ego), it certainly shows he or she is not stodgy.

You may come across a sample of writing where there are unique capital "I" formations, other than those mentioned here, and those capitals will need to be analyzed according to the rest of the signs in the handwriting. It is not possible to show every formation here, but the dozen "I" specimens illustrated here are a good basis for understanding that letter.

CHAPTER FIFTEEN

Formations of Small Letters

The shape of the letters may be round or angular, or variations of either form. A child may be taught to make rounded formations (either in the cursive or the manuscript method of penmanship), yet on reaching adulthood many of these round forms become angular; this shows the individuality of the personality is expressing itself.

Generally the shapes of the letters fall into four classifications:

1. rounded
2. angular
3. garland many
4. threading

1. Round (called arcade)
2. Angular (points where curves should be)
3. Garland ("u" and "n" and "m" look alike)
4. Threading (the letters trail into a thin line)

ROUND LETTERS

The round letters, in arcade or arched form, accompanied with round capitals, indicate a nonaggressive personality. This person does not like to get into arguments and prefers to work cooperatively with others rather than to assume heavy responsibilities alone.

There is not much spontaneity in the rounded writing, and the writer may be quite gullible. It is usually not hard to understand the person who writes with rounded forms, as there may not be much subtlety in his personality makeup, and the writer is usually consistent.

Light pressure in rounded handwriting shows gentleness; whereas heavy pressure in rounded formations may mean the person is not so gentle and may want to be self-assertive, but still has all the other traits found in the rounded handwriting. Rounded handwriting done with a very light pressure is usually the sign of a conformist, who tries not to cause any dissension.

If the rounded small letters are accompanied by angular capitals, this shows the outer manner may seem aggressive, yet the inner person is not really so sure of himself and possesses the traits which are found in round handwriting. Those angular capital letters are merely a facade to impress people with a self-assurance which may not really exist.

When rounded handwriting is large and regular, in almost a precision-made manner, and is written with heavy pressure, the person wants to be independent and go ahead on his own. But this is not so, as the arcade forms still show a lack of sufficient aggressiveness to allow for individual action.

The very small writing which is made of rounded formations is not often seen. It is an interesting combination of a mind that is inquiring and able to deal with details and facts, plus a cooperative and sympathetic nature. The heart is tender, but the mind is acute.

ANGULAR LETTERS

In writing which shows many angles (where normally we expect to see curves) the indication is that the personality is aggressive. The writer wants to assert his own views, pursue his own activities, without needing to cooperate with or be answerable to other people. The angular writer is not too easy to understand, not too easy to please, as he is not gullible nor too loquacious (especially when it comes to talking about his own ideas or feelings).

Angular writing indicates a critical mind, and often the writer is more interested in facts, in things, in work, rather than in other people. The one who writes with angular formations is often more discriminating in "hand-picking" his close friends than is the person who writes with rounded forms.

Usually the angular writer is practical and has shrewd judgment in handling his financial matters. He may have a keen interest in business life; or, in a professional career, he may be interested in work which requires an analytical approach or the use of hands in some skillful manner.

Angular letters which are large and have a heavy pressure show the person to be aggressive and ambitious. The writer does not want to be subordinated to anyone, in his work or in personal life; he does not want to be placed in a situation where he needs to make any compromise, and he is usually shrewd in knowing when to take advantage of a promising opportunity.

When the angular handwriting is very small but clear, it signifies a mind that is keen, and this person is inclined to be a specialist in whatever field he pursues. He does not take anything for granted, he analyzes each detail of his work, he prefers to get down to basics and not rely on superficialities or hearsay. This small, angular writing shows the person does not need social life on a widespread scale; the preference is for just a small group of people with whom common interests and goals may be shared.

But should the angular writing be very small and squeezed tightly together, the capitals tightly cramped, the "o" and "a" and "g" tied up tightly, the graphologist finds here the person who is unduly concerned about money matters, to the point where he may be a penny-pincher. It is usually hard to communicate with this person, as his attitude is full of skepticism. Also, he may be most secretive about himself.

Angular writing which shows many tasteful printed letter forms, which are distinctive but simple, is a sign of a constructive mind. Often it shows a person who can use his hands in some constructive manner. These people may be most interesting as companions; yet the angular formations show they have the critical and often standoffish traits which are common to most angular writers, so the appeal to these people must be through the intellect and not directly to the emotions.

Sometimes an angular writing has large, irregular formations and perhaps eccentric capitals. This person is usually concerned with his own self, without much consideration for the other fellow. Among such writers we often find the so-called temperamental artist and actor.

A person who writes with angular forms may be deeply in love, may be very romantic; yet does not show the inner feelings in as demonstrative a manner as the one who writes with rounded formations.

When the American graphologist is given a specimen of angular handwriting, and recognizes the penmanship to be either German or of some other foreign country where angular penmanship is taught in school, it may be necessary to "discount" half the angles and analyze the handwriting from the other signs which are evident.

GARLAND LETTERS

This is the writing where the "n" and "m" resemble the "u" and "w" and the arcades are reversed; the rounded formations are on the base line and the points are on top. It may seem hard to read at first if the letters are not too clear or are too quickly written; but once the handwriting analyst's eye gets used to it, the garland writing is easy to understand.

The outstanding trait in a garland handwriting is the person's desire to live in a luxurious manner and not to have to work hard to earn the money to pay for the luxuries. The garland writer is a pleasure-loving individual. But if it is necessary for this person to work for a living, he or she will usually look for a job that has a touch of "glamour" to it, where the surroundings are attractive and where there is a chance to meet interesting people, and perhaps to have a good social life as a "fringe benefit" of the job.

The one who writes with garland forms is usually an imitator rather than an innovator. It is much easier to function that way! Sometimes a person who writes with garlands may work hard, or may live modestly; but this does not mean that he or she prefers that, and if there were enough money, this same person would find it very gratifying to shift over to easy and gracious living patterns.

The garland writers usually have outer manners which are gracious; consciously they have a need to impress other people, so they may use tact and "put on an act" and appear to be much more interested in some people and activities than perhaps they really are. It is important to the garland writer to be noticed and admired, because usually that person does not possess as much real self-assurance as may appear on the surface.

THREADING LETTERS

The words are written in a threadlike sprawl rather than in a rounded, angular, or garland form. The pen hardly seems to touch the sheet of paper on which the writing appears. This is a difficult sign for the graphologist to figure out in a hurry, and the analysis of the writing must really depend on all the other contributing signs to be able to deduce whether the threadline writing may be due to excessive haste and impatience, or if there are some inner tensions and conflicts between the head and the heart. Or, the threading may be due to intuition or to lack of convention, to the writer's being a nonconformist, or perhaps to his wish to get away from anything unpleasant. Or, it may be versatility and intellectual creativeness.

There is no one sign which may be applied to the threading letters, so the analyst must leave that to the last, after all other indications in the handwriting are examined.

CLOSED OR OPEN LETTERS

Some letters are naturally formed with closings, but some writers may leave them open or they may tie them up very closely. Most generally the "a," "o," "b," and "g" belong in this group.

1. a o b g

2. a o b g

3. a o b g

4. a o b g

1. The letter is lightly closed, and it shows a person who will have confidence in others, though not in a gullible manner.

2. If the letter is not merely closed, but is tied with a knot, it reveals the person to be very cautious, hesitant to

tell anything to anyone, and just as hesitant to believe all he sees or hears. This person has to be thoroughly convinced in his own mind that a new idea or plan is right, before he will proceed with it.

3. When the letters are open, they usually express gullibility; the writer has a trusting nature and is willing to share his thoughts and affections and worldly goods with others. It is wise not to confide secrets to this person, because he may (with all good intention, and not maliciously) tell them to someone else.

4. It is rare to see the letter with a break in the bottom of the round circle. In fact, it is sometimes spotted only when a magnifying glass is used. This is not a pleasant sign, as it reveals the person who might be too easily tempted away from the straight-and-narrow path (especially in matters of the petty cash box). However, the novice graphologist is warned not to jump to conclusions here and not to express such a finding unless there is absolute assurance to back it up. Sometimes this break may be due to a faulty pen, to a thick and rough texture of the paper, or to weak and runny ink. Also, if this sign appears only once, or once in a while, it may not have significance; but if it repeats itself throughout the person's handwriting, then one should be on the alert against such a weak personality trait.

INTROVERTED LETTERS

When a letter is done by writing from right to left, rather than the natural movement of the pen from left to right, we may find signs of the introvert.

1. Here we see the letters as they should naturally be

written, starting from the left and going forward toward the right.

2. But these letters are written by being pulled back to the left.

1. b d D y

2. b d D y

There may be other letter forms in a handwriting which are "pulled to the left" when they should go to the right; but these serve to show how this introverted sign may be recognized. They are usually found in a backhand writing, though sometimes they do appear in a handwriting which slants toward the right (showing that that person may be an extrovert, yet does have some innate introverted tendencies which have not been overcome).

In these cases of conflicting signs the judgment and experience of the trained graphologist has to be carefully exercized before the final analysis is made.

"CULTURED" LETTERS

The handwriting may possess some unusual forms of letters which are known as the cultured signs or as Greek letters.

1. The "d" which ends with its stem brought over to the left and the "g" which resembles the number "8" are

often found in the handwritings of people of intellectual minds and activities.

We may sometimes see such letters in handwritings which do not bear out the signs of culture; in such a case

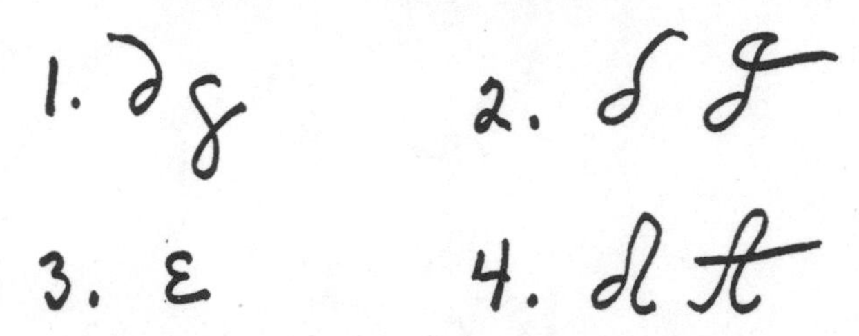

the graphologist must study them well to see if they are not merely fakes or if they are truly part of the writing. An uncultured person might be told that a Greek "d" or "g" shows culture, and he might then incorporate them in his writing just to show off. But it does not take the trained handwriting analyst long to discern if they are fake or real. If they are real, then we know this person does have a feeling for the intellectual part of life and may be striving toward such achievement.

2. When the stem on the Greek "d" does not remain simple, but comes back and ends at the right, with or without an added knot to it, it is an unnecessary flourish and it indicates that this person may have superficial qualities of intellect rather than innate ones.

3. The "e" which looks like the reverse of the numeral "3" may sometimes be included in a handwriting which contains both the Greek "d" and the "g." In such a case, the graphologist accepts this as an additional mark of culture. But if the "e" appears by itself (without the accompaniment of the "d" and the "g"), it may just mean the person is making a try at being cultivated but may not necessarily

be so. In addition, if the "e" is by itself, it shows the writer wants to be in surroundings where there are people and things of "glamour" and where he or she may shine by reflection of such personalities.

4. The straddle "d" and "t" are often a puzzlement to the graphologist. This belongs to the person who does not betray a trust, who is cautious in choosing suitable companions and surroundings. When these formations appear in a handwriting which has other signs of intellectual quality, they enhance that significance. But should they appear in a writing which does not show any other outstanding traits, they may mean just plain secretiveness which is not backed by intellectual reasoning.

ENLARGED SMALL LETTERS

The letter "r" may be written much larger than the other small letters in a word. This shows the writer loves to

hard bemoan

create a fine appearance in clothes and jewelry. The enlarged "r" is often found in the handwritings of fashion models and of women and men who enjoy shopping for attractive wearing apparel for themselves. Also, the writer with the large "r" usually likes an interesting social life. This formation is found more in the handwritings of the extroverts, rather than in introverted writing.

When the "m" and the "n" are made larger than the other small letters, they reveal a desire to be in a managerial post (in a job, or in personal life). Also, as explained in Chapter XIV about the capital letters "M" and "N," when the first "loop" in the small letter "m" or "n" is higher than the next one, it accentuates the writer's desire to exercize his executive ability.

VARIATIONS IN LETTER FORMS

If in one person's handwriting you find all sorts of small letter formations, perhaps the "s" made in three different ways, or the "l" or "j" or other letters made in various ways, it will be necessary to make a most patient analysis of each sign of the handwriting (such as the size, slant, pressure, etc.), and then determine why the letter form variations occur.

In some cases they may indicate lack of concentration, in others they may show versatility, impatience, originality, carelessness, or many other underlying causes for the diversification of the formation styles. Irregularity and variation in letter forms is a result, not a cause.

CHAPTER SIXTEEN

The "i" Dot and the "t" Bar

The little dot over the "i" and the crossing stroke through the "t" may seem such insignificant things in a handwriting, yet they have a good deal of meaning. There are undoubtedly as many different "i" dots and "t" bars as there are people in the world; each handwriting portrays each individual person. So we cannot discuss every sort of dot and crossing here, but we will show those most generally used.

In some handwritings you may find a dozen different "i" dots or "t" bars. It is necessary to keep count of them, to see which appear more often and which appear only once (or hardly ever). For instance, you may find one circular "i" dot and twelve plain ones right over the letter; you know then that the one circular dot (which will be explained in the following illustration) does not have too much significance, because the dozen plain dots are more plentiful. Or, you may see one big, dashing "t" bar (also explained in the following illustration) plus ten small halfway bars which don't go through the stem of the letter itself. Thus you may deduce that the one dashing "t" crossing doesn't have much significance, because the nine halfway crossing bars are more dominant. So, with these variable dots and dashes, you will simply have to do adding or subtracting to find which trait is the dominant one and which a slightly passive one.

If in the handwriting sample you find that the "i" is not dotted and the "t" is not crossed, it may mean the writer is absent-minded or lacks concentration. If the dot or the crossing-stroke is omitted only once, it is not important to attach too much significance to that one omission; however, if the "i" dots and the "t" crossings never appear, then it is essential to pay heed to that sign. The writer may have a good memory for big things but may not pay much attention to small details.

MEANING OF "i" DOTS

1. The small, light-pressure dot which is properly placed over the letter reveals a person who is careful with details, likes to be punctual, and does not allow enthusiasms to run away with him.

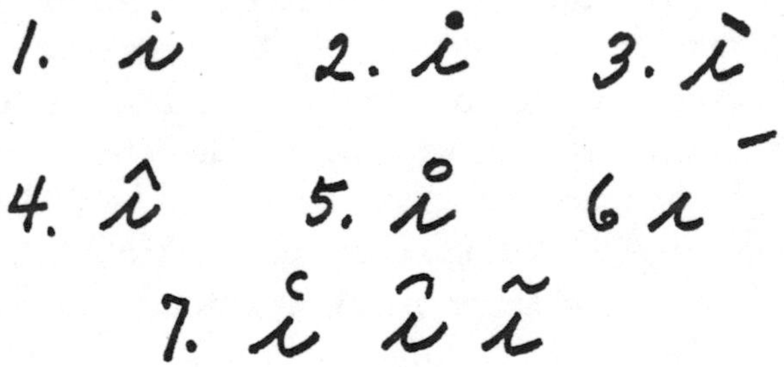

2. When this small kind of dot is made with a heavy pressure, it has the same meaning as the preceding one, except here the writer is more positive in his thinking and more self-assertive.

3. The dot which points downward in a blunt manner, and has heavy pressure, shows the writer to have a stubborn streak. This person is not gullible and usually has fixed opinions.

4. When the "i" has a little tent-shaped dot over it, we find a critical mind, and there is often subtlety and a keen wit. This person likes to get down to basics and usually analyzes all new ideas and all new people.

5. The little circle over the "i" (often also used as a period after a sentence) shows the person who might like to lead an unconventional life (but the other signs in the handwriting would have to show whether there is enough self-confidence to do so). This circle-dot indicates a desire for beauty in surroundings and in clothes. Sometimes this person has a flair for art and might be able to express his taste for color and design. But he may not really have the ability to do creative work, so usually he remains the adapter of art rather than the innovator. Of course, there is often a bit of a joker in this circle-dot which the graphologist may be able to catch. It may appear in a handwriting that is loaded with flamboyant, ornamented formations, and the circle "i" dot might then just be a mark of the show-off personality rather than indicative of a true flair for artistic things.

6. The dashing "i" dot (not really a dot, but more of a dash) which is flung very high above the letter itself, sometimes to the right of it, sometimes to the left, signifies much enthusiasm. The writer has imagination, may like to try out fun ideas, and may get bored with any routine task made up of sameness of details.

7. You may not be able to see these wavy, funny little marks which take the place of dots. Your magnifying glass

comes in handy here, and you may find tiny crescent moons, little semicircles, wiggly forms of all sorts. These show the writer has a sense of humor, and the more variable and unusual the little "dot" forms, the greater may be the sense of mimicry when this person tells a funny story. Such a writer usually does not take himself too seriously and adapts to the situation whatever it might be.

THE CROSSING STROKES OF "t"

1. When the "t" bar is in proportion to the letter and crosses its stem at the proper place, it shows the writer is calm, has good control over the emotions, does not rush ahead on impulse, and pays attention to all details.

1. t 2. t 3. t 4. t

5. t 6. t 7. t

8. t 9. t 10. t

11. t 12. t 13. that

14. titter 15. that

16. t 17. t

(Generally this person also dots the "i" right over the letter, as shown in Item 1 in the foregoing section on "i" dots.)

2. Here is the procrastinator! The bar starts on its journey, gets to the stem of the "t" and stops. A person who does this may sometimes impress upon others that he has loads of new ideas, but the chances are he won't go through with them if he makes these "t" bars.

3. The crossing stroke is short, blunt, and points downward. This person has a very critical mind as well as a stubborn way of holding on to his own ideas. You cannot convince this person, as there is not a bit of flexibility about taking notice of other people's ideas. (Usually this writer also makes the blunt "i" dot shown in Item 3 in the section on "i" dots.)

4. The stroke which goes to the letter, but not through it, shows this person to be a procrastinator. In addition, the pressure is heavy and the line is pointed downward; this adds a critical attitude to the procrastinating one.

5. While this "t" does not have a bar going through it, it is considered to be crossed, as the upward stroke to the right of the "t" does finish it off. When this kind of "t" is written most of the time, it shows a conventional person who has a respect for tradition, and it also may mean a lack of initiative. However, if it just appears once in a while, it may not be significant, as it is only a throwback to the early days of school when this form was taught as part of the Palmer cursive method.

6. A long "t" bar which goes straight across is a sign of self-assertion; the writer likes to aim for success in all undertakings and is not easily discouraged.

7. The same long stroke with a very heavy pressure

(heavier than the rest of the writing) means the same as the preceding one; however, this shows more forceful will power.

8. Here is the romantic "t" bar. This person likes social activities and is usually conventional (even though he may be interested in new trends).

9. When the "t" is tied up with a knot, it reveals a tenacious person, one who can hold on to an idea or a task until he finds the result he seeks or voluntarily wishes to give it up.

10. The high-flying stroke over the "t" is a sign of imagination, enthusiasm, and sometimes a reaching out for the unattainable. (This person usually makes the "i" dots which fly high over the letter, as shown in Item 6 in the foregoing section on "i" dots.)

11. The long "t" bar shows the writer aspires to success; however, as this starts high but slants downward and ends low, it shows he is ambitious for material success. He is "coming down to earth."

12. But when the long bar aims high, starting low and then slanting upward, it shows the ambition is not completely practical or material. There is also an aim for spiritual satisfaction. This one is "reaching for the sky."

13. In a cursive writing you may find the printed "t" formation, either connected to the letter which follows it or disconnected. This shows a resourceful, constructive mind. (You may find other printed formations coming into the cursive writing when the person makes these printed "t" forms.)

14. If a word has two or more "t's" in it, and there is just one line drawn through (instead of three small, separate "t" bars), it shows the person thinks quickly and

tries out shortcuts with all new ideas. Here the writer was able to accomplish three operations with only one stroke of the pen.

15. When the writer makes a big loop and ties it up like a lasso, it indicates a very persistent person who clings to his possessions and his viewpoints. He may be interested in the opinions of others, but he won't let go of his own.

16. When a little umbrella covers the top of the "t," it reveals control over emotions. This is often found in the handwriting of people who prefer to be alone at times and do serious thinking about new ideas. It may also hide the fact that the person is more emotional than appears on the surface, and the curved stroke is a way of "covering up" inner feelings.

17. This curved line goes upward, in reverse to the preceding one. When you find a "t" which has this unusual method of crossing the letter, it indicates the writer to have sensitive responses to people and surroundings, and the mind is imaginative. This person is prone to being influenced by people who have aggressively dominant personalities, as he is desirous of maintaining a sense of harmony in all human relationships and does not feel it important to get into dissension.

CHAPTER SEVENTEEN

Beginning and Ending Strokes

The beginning stroke leading into the first letter of a word and the ending stroke tagged on to the last letter are carefully made when the child first learns to write. Some adults make these strokes forever, and some eliminate either the beginning or the final stroke or both strokes.

1. This person does not take chances with new ideas or activities. The beginning stroke is the preliminary "thinking it over" period before starting anything new. This usually denotes a conventional person, who does not take on aggressive or competitive activities but prefers to function cooperatively with others.

2. When the beginning stroke is eliminated it shows the writer does not need to make the "leading into the word" gesture, and is able to discard nonessential ideas, things, and actions in getting to a desired goal. The beginning stroke is not really necessary in order to form the first letter in the word; the more nonessential strokes a writer eliminates, the more direct and resourceful is his approach to new ideas.

3. The long, curved final strokes show a desire for social life; when this person chooses a job, he wants to be in surroundings where there is congeniality among the

people he meets. These final strokes also indicate a conventional attitude, and a sense of humor (if the "i" dots are made in funny, wiggly shapes as explained in Chapter XVI).

1. c a t
2. c a t
3. m s t
4. m t r
5. m r
6. m s
7. this

4. The abrupt final stroke, done in a downward manner, discloses the writer to be self-assertive and to have definite opinions about people and things. If the stroke is done with light pressure, it shows a sensitive person who (while possessing these definite traits) may not take a strong stand against other people. But if the pressure of the

final stroke is very heavy (often heavier than the rest of the word), it means the person may be belligerent when upholding a personal opinion.

5. A long straight final stroke reveals self-confidence. The degree of this confidence is seen in the length and the pressure of the final stroke. If it is written with light pressure, and appears in a rounded handwriting, the self-confidence is not pushed forward in a domineering manner. But if the final stroke is written with a heavier pressure than the word itself, and if it is in an angular handwriting, it shows a more forceful personality than the one with light pressure. While this person may not always put individual ideas in motion, the desire is to work by himself and not necessarily to share everything with others. Also, there is the desire to be a forerunner and not merely a follower.

6. The final stroke which is done with a downward curve shows the person to be stubborn, but not in a fixed manner. There is flexibility in this stroke; the writer is generally a conformist even though there may be a tendency to want to do things which are different from the usual conventional pattern.

7. A final stroke which comes back and under the word in an exaggeratedly long tail reveals a desire for attention. Even though other signs in the handwriting might point to introversion, this large ending stroke shows the writer is not only content to achieve things but also wants to be applauded for whatever he does accomplish.

PERSISTENT HOOKS AND KNOTS IN LETTER FORMS

Instead of an actual beginning and final stroke, we find hooks and knots in some handwritings. In some cases it is necessary to use the magnifying glass to verify the little hooks. They show up especially on the ends of the "t" crossing bar and on capital letters. A hook or a knot is a sign of persistence; it latches on to a letter formation as a sign of the person's mind latching on to some idea and holding on to it.

1. how is
2. how is
3. Here this
4. knot o a

1. The hooks which appear at the beginning of a word show stubbornness; but this is not carried out to an extreme, and usually the persistence is about small matters. This person is not too set in his ways, and he may come over to the other fellow's way of thinking if the matter is carefully explained to him.

2. When there is no hook at the beginning of the word, but we find a hook at the end of it, the person might appear to be most cooperative when a new idea is expounded or a new task has to be started; however, the final hook shows he may not carry through on the other fellow's idea, and he may become stubborn. Also, he may start his own plan in not too self-assured a manner; but, as he proceeds and sees the thing taking shape, he usually

develops a more persistent attitude, and it is not easy to budge this person once his mind becomes set.

3. When the tenacious hooks are made both at the start and the end of a word or a crossing stroke, as shown in this "H" and "t", here is the one who starts out with a stubborn attitude and maintains it all the time he is working on a new idea. He is hard to convince and will only accept the concepts of others if he first studies them and feels they may be of advantage to him.

4. Knots are also signs of stubbornness; but they may also be indications of secretiveness. The knots show the person may become too tied up in trivial details which may not deserve so much attention, and which may hinder him from going ahead as quickly as he might.

Generally, a rounded and large handwriting does not possess these little hooks and knots; we find them mostly in angular and small handwritings. The one who writes with rounded, large formations is usually more gregarious than the one with angular, small writing; thus, the former is more apt to want to please people (to be in their good graces) and so may give in more easily than the one who writes with angular, small letters.

The graphologist does not always consider the hooks and knots as faulty traits. There are times when all other signs in the writing show the person to be gullible and not sufficiently self-assured; and in such a case the stubborn streak may add a bit of "backbone" to the thoughts and actions of this writer.

CHAPTER EIGHTEEN

Zones and Loops

A handwriting consists of three zones: upper, middle, lower. The letters which reach into the upper zone are the "l," "h," "d," "t," and capital letters. In the lower zone we find "g," "y," "q," "p," "z," "j." The "f" appears both in the upper and lower zones.

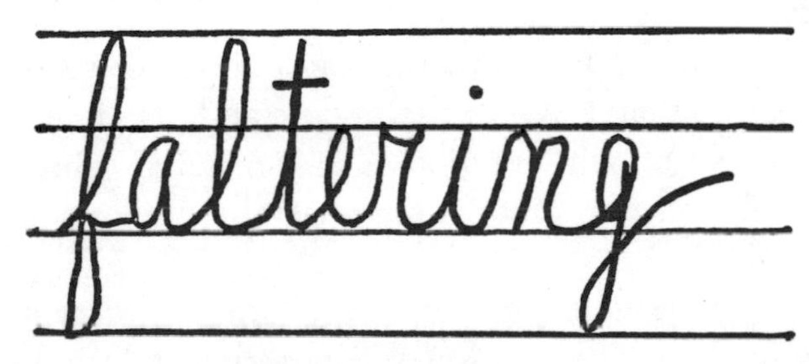

The significance of the relationship in size of the letters in all three zones was given much study in 1930 by Professor Max Pulver of the University of Switzerland, enabling graphologists to make a clearer analysis of the upper and lower loops which appear in the writing.

UPPER, MIDDLE, LOWER ZONES

1. Loops in the upper zone, which are proportionately too tall for the middle and lower zones, generally show

1. high loops

2. hay leg

3. where you lay

high aspirations. These may be toward idealism, spirituality, or other reaching-up for things which are not materialistic.

2. When the letters in the lower zone are proportionately larger than those in the middle and upper zones, we find the person who is ambitious for material gain, who is practical, and the interests are generally earthy ones (not spiritual).

3. If the middle zone letters are larger in proportion to those in the upper and lower zones, the writer is subjectively concerned with his own interests, with everyday matters in human relationships and work. He does not reach too high into the objective or spiritual realm of aspiration, nor too deeply into the physical or material ambitions. This person likes to be on safe ground and not reach out from the realities of his daily life. The middle-zone writer may get into certain patterns of thought and action, which may turn into fixed habits.

When a handwriting is well proportioned in all three zones, it reveals a person who functions in a balanced way;

he recognizes the realities of everyday life (the middle zone), he has an imagination (upper zone) which is disciplined, and he keeps his physical and material appetites (the lower zone) in control.

LOOPS IN UPPER AND LOWER ZONES

If there is a variety of loops (in the upper, lower, or both zones), it indicates the writer's tendency to fluctuate in aspirations and ambitions according to the variability of his moods.

1. hag 2. hag 3. hag
4. hag 5. hag 6. hay
7. hag

1. The tall, narrow loop shows spiritual aspirations, and if it appears in a rounded, good-sized handwriting, it usually shows clannishness, and caution in proceeding with new ideas even though there may be an urge to try them out. But if this loop is in a handwriting that is angular, in rather small formations, it shows the aspira-

tions are toward intellectual aims, and the writer may be more inclined to take a chance than the one with the rounded writing.

An interesting discovery was made by Louise Rice, about thirty years ago, in regard to these tall, narrow loops. She studied many handwritings of young men who were entering the field of aviation, and in most cases she found the tall "reaching up to the skies" loops. I have found this, too, following Louise Rice's study of this, and while the tall loop is not in all flyers' handwritings, it does show up quite frequently.

These tall upper loops are often found in the handwritings of religious people, and sometimes of those who are superstitious and whose whole attitudes may be "out of this world" and who may find it hard to stay on a mundane level.

2. When the tall loop is inflated, it also shows high aspirations, but not as spiritual in essence as the preceding tall narrow letter. While this person may be as clannish as the preceding one, he also likes to widen his social circle.

3. The upper-zone loop which is made short in proportion to the rest of the writing shows the person does not permit his aspirations to run too high, and is quite cautious about letting the mind soar to any new ideas or to go on any flights of fancy. In a writing which has small angular formations, this short upper loop shows the writer is able to concentrate well and sticks to factual things rather than letting his imagination play much part in his ideas.

4. When the lower loop is inflated, it is a sign of gaiety, a desire to be with interesting people and in attractive surroundings, and to avoid work or social activities which are too routine. This writer generally has material ambition, and he also may enjoy physical activity in sports or

dancing. The person may "talk a good line of idealism" but actually he will usually find it easier to be an idealist when his material needs are fully satisfied. The larger the lower loop, the more "down to earth" is the personality.

5. If the lower loop is short in proportion to the handwriting, it reveals the person who prefers to work cooperatively with others rather than to go on his own initiative. The manner is not an outgoing one, and the writer usually waits for someone else to take the lead before voicing his own viewpoints or showing his innermost feelings. He is not ambitious beyond what he feels are his limitations, he does not aspire to great heights nor to material gain. If necessary he gets along on a modest budget. He is usually easy to understand, and there is no guile in this writer.

6. When you see a loop which is an incurve at the end of the letter, it is to be considered the same as a hook, which is discussed in Chapter XVII. This is just a large-sized hook, showing the writer to have tenacity of purpose.

7. The upper and lower loops are inflated, showing an exaggeration of the aspirations toward intellectual and idealistic matters, as well as the desire for physical and material satisfactions. This writer usually wants to live on a scale of grandeur, wants to do and have things for the sake of personal aggrandizement. The inflated loops show a distaste for any work or social activities which would prove confining. The personality is usually a vital one, and the writer desires to make a good impression on others.

ELIMINATION OF LOOPS

Instead of a loop the letters in the upper and lower zones may often be made with straight lines. They look like printed formations in a cursive handwriting and are often accompanied by other printed forms in the specimen of writing.

1. boy   2. boy

1. The person whose mind wants to be uncluttered, who wishes to eliminate nonessentials and get everything down to a simple formula, is the one who is most likely to eliminate the curved beginning and ending stroke on the upper and lower loops. There is nothing pretentious in this personality, the mind is resourceful, and if necessary to adapt to a new situation this person can usually find a way of doing it.

2. Here the writer makes heavy, blunt strokes. Essentially the same traits apply to this one as to the preceding writer; but this person may be more opinionated and not so ready to accept or adapt to the ideas of others without first putting them through a critical test.

PULLED-BACK LOOPS

The neophyte graphologist may sometimes overlook the unusual formation in a handwriting, without realizing that often it is this difference in formation which might hold a strong clue. For example:

heavy heavy heavy

If a loop in the lower or upper zone pulls in the opposite direction from the other formations in the writing, it may be a sign of introversion, or hesitation to cooperate with others, or a resentment. Of course the other signs in the handwriting must be judged before the final analysis is made; but it is well to be on guard about a loop which pulls away from the rest of the word.

UNCOMMON LOOPS

The loops (especially the lower ones) are often a temptation for the writer to attempt some fancy ornamentation. The more the writer adds unnecessary strokes to the loop, the more his mind is crowded with nonessentials; whereas the simpler the formations, the more the person gets down to basics.

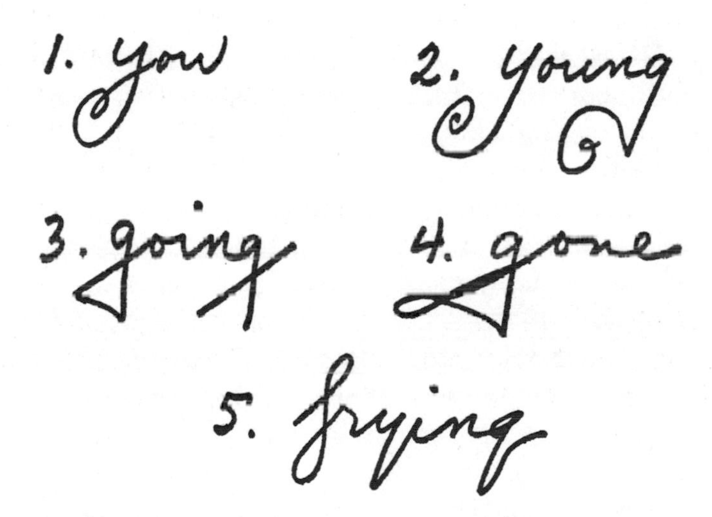

1. The loop which ties a knot in itself shows a personality that may not be too easy to understand, as this writer

may have some unique ideas of his own. He may pride himself on having an independent mind, but it may often shut itself too strongly against the ideas of others. Stubbornness is indicated when there is a knotted loop.

2. The curlicues on ends of loops often take artistic shapes, but usually they are just cluttered formations. This may be analyzed in the same manner as the preceding one (the knotted loop); but the more complicated the ornamentation may become, the more complex this person's mind might be.

3. By itself the angular loop, if it appears in a handwriting which is done with angular formations, has no special meaning; except it might show a strong self-assertiveness. But if the angular loop appears in a writing with rounded formations, the person is not too assertive, and this angular loop may just be a sign of a mild stubbornness when it is necessary to hold on to an opinion.

Notice the "g" at the end of the word "going" in the illustration; while it is open at the bottom, it is regarded as the angular formation.

4. The angular loop which has a knot in it has the same essential meaning as the preceding one (without the knot); however, this tied-in knot is just an extra bit of persistence and perhaps some exaggeration of the writer's own ideas.

5. These loops are written in reverse; that is, on the bottom "f" loop instead of the pen going down and then coming up on the right and closing in the middle of the letter toward the left, the pen comes down, turns left, and then goes up and crosses to the right. The loops on the "y" and "g" make the upstroke to the right of the letter rather than to the left and through; the "g" resembles the letter

"q." The same meaning attaches to all three letters; these are the altruistic loops; the writer understands human nature and is broad-minded in his attitudes toward all people. The altruistic letter formations reveal the person who wants to be of aid to others; sometimes the writer may have no money to give away, but does have understanding and in other ways may be helpful. An added quality in these altruistic forms is that the person may usually be able to express himself with fluency, in writing or in speech.

CHAPTER NINETEEN

Signatures and Punctuation

A graphologist hesitates to analyze a signature unless it is accompanied by a few lines of handwriting, for the reason that often the signature is stylized and does not resemble the writing. Some people may use two or more different signatures; one is the natural one for signing personal letters, etc., and the other is devised for business papers and bank checks, or perhaps just to impress others with a distinctive signature.

For example, a handwriting may be small and angular but the signature may be large and round. This reveals an outer personality (the signature) which is gregarious, and the writer thus impresses people; yet the handwriting itself shows a reserved person, careful with details.

In reverse, the handwriting may be large and round but the signature small and angular. In this case the outer personality shown to the public is one of reserve and caution; whereas the inner personality is a friendly one and likes to be with people.

SIGNATURE IS OUTER EXPRESSION

Another case might be where the writing is backhand (meaning the person is an introvert), yet the signature may be written in a right-hand slant. Here the outer personality impresses itself on others as outgoing and extroverted; however, the inner personality is hesitant about entering into new relationships or undertaking unfamiliar ideas and tasks.

But if the signature is backhand, and the rest of the handwriting slants to the right, we find the reverse. Here the person acts in an aloof manner, hiding the fact that he is really gregarious and is just putting on a cold manner to keep people from coming too close (unless he wants them to do so).

The same holds true of heavy pressure versus light pressure and of all other signs in the handwriting itself which may be shown as completely opposite in the signature.

A graphologist will often be given a typewritten letter with only the signature written in script; this is usually from someone who has a top job or is in public life. The chance is that this person is so busy that his signature is written by his private secretary and not by himself. So the analysis would hardly be fair!

Also, an autograph on a photograph of a celebrity is sometimes submitted to the handwriting analyst; here the name may have been signed by someone who is hired to do so and not by the famous personality himself. It is best not to attempt an analysis of such a signature without procuring some of the handwriting of the person.

THE LINE UNDER THE SIGNATURE

An interesting significance may be found in the way the signature is underlined. Generally, the underscore is prompted by the person wanting to assert himself, wanting to receive recognition from others.

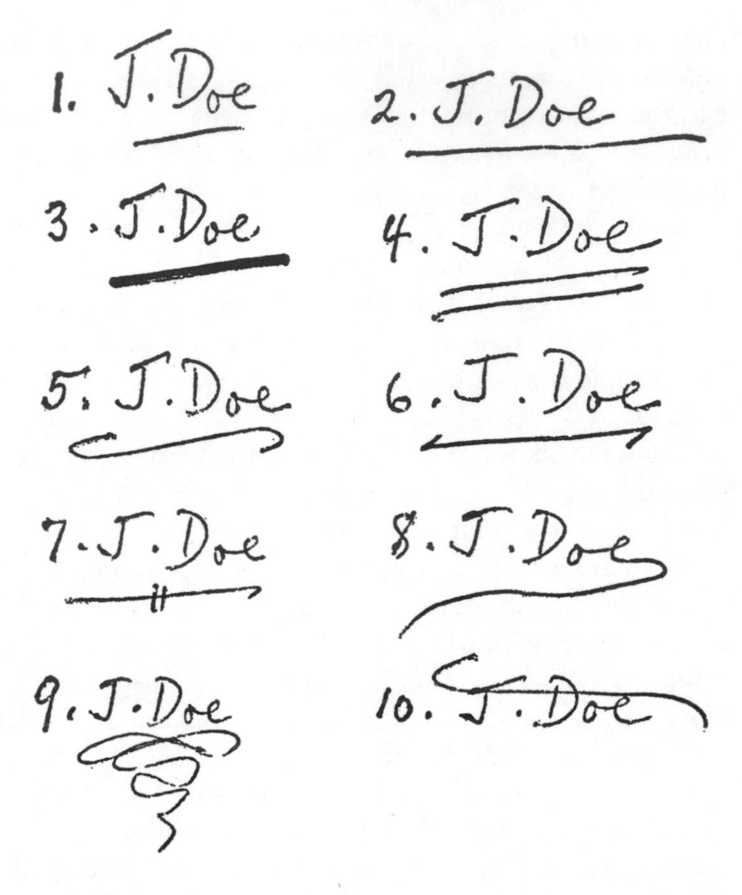

1. The small line under the name is self-assertion, as all underscoring of a signature is; however, this is not an overbearing attitude on the writer's part, and it is more a matter of pride than of conceit.

2. When the straight line goes under the entire signature, and is done with a light pressure of the pen, it is a matter of pride and self-confidence, and this writer likes to be noticed (but not necessarily flattered).

3. Should the straight line be written with heavy pres-

sure it shows a more aggressive attitude than the preceding one, and there is more of a desire for acclaim and for material gain.

4. If there are two lines in the underscore, it reveals the writer's desire to be top man in all social and business activities.

5. The gracious host may make this curved line under his name; it is a romantic sign, and the writer wants to be admired and applauded. Also, there is an appreciation for beautiful things in this curved stroke.

6. The ambitious person may make angular forms on the line which underscores the signature. He has much self-assurance and does not give up too easily once the mind is set on reaching a goal.

7. The two little dots or lines in the center of the underscoring are really a symbol of the "dollar sign." This person likes to think about money; he may not have money and may never earn it or get it; but he likes it, and he has shrewd instincts where finances are concerned.

8. When the underscore is made in a continuous line from the name itself, it reveals the person not only to be self-assertive but also persistent. If the writing of the name and its underscoring is of light pressure and the curve of the stroke is graceful, the person is not harsh or aggressive toward others. But if this kind of underscoring is in an angular writing and has a heavy pressure, then it shows an ambitious drive and persistence. Actually, this type of ending of the signature is like a big hook, a sign of persistence.

9. The elaborate underscoring is not always too clear a sign for the graphologist to comprehend, so the analysis must be made from the rest of the handwriting, and there

the analyst may find the clue to why such a complicated underscoring is made. However, it is safe to assume that in such a case the person is desirous of receiving much admiration and attention for whatever he achieves or acquires.

10. Here we have an overline and not an underline. This is not very common, but occasionally it does occur. The writer has original ideas and may be slightly eccentric. However, it is not really easy to know why the line goes above rather than below the signature, and it is best for the graphologist to play it safe and analyze the handwriting formations and not pay too much heed to the signature or its overline.

USE OF EXCESSIVE PUNCTUATION

Rarely you will find a period after a signature; it is not grammatically essential to do so. The period may mean caution, or it may mean defiance, dependent on the rest of the signs in the handwriting. If it's done in a handwriting which shows mildness and lack of self-assertiveness, the period after the name may be accepted as a mark of caution. But if the period after the signature appears in a handwriting which shows aggressiveness and self-assurance, then that period may be translated as a mark of defiance.

Usually, when the period after the signature is called to the attention of the person who makes it, he or she will be astounded, as there is no awareness on the part of the writer that it is being done. That period after the name is an unconscious gesture.

In the body of the handwriting (aside from the signature) there may appear an exaggerated amount and style of punctuation. Instead of a comma or a dot there may appear a dash or a series of dashes. Many of the words may be underlined (when they do not need to be). Exclamation points may be used instead of periods and sometimes may appear in the middle of a word. An abundance of quotation marks and parentheses may be placed around words and phrases. Asterisks may float all over the page.

When the sheet of handwriting is overloaded with excess quotation marks, the writer is inclined to dramatize every trivial thing, and this might be an outer manifestation of an inner enthusiasm which just has to express itself. A lack of concentration is also read into this tendency to overpunctuate. Such a person craves excitement and a change of pace at all times.

CHAPTER TWENTY

How Do You Doodle?

A doodle is a scribble, especially the kind you draw while you're sitting at the telephone and making all sorts of little pictures and diagrams on the note pad. Many interesting doodles are made by people sitting in at business conferences, and the results of their scribblings bear no relationship to the topic they are discussing. The doodle is an unconscious expression of the inner self, and often it is a surprise to the graphologist or to any other person in the field of psychology who makes a study of people's doodles.

The person whose manner seems so aggressive may doodle delicate little figures; the woman on the telephone who is ordering groceries from the market may be drawing musical notes; the sweet little woman may be doodling big animals or large structural patterns.

The graphologist prefers not to make an analysis only from the doodles, but wants to have a sample of the person's handwriting as well. However, it is interesting to read meanings in these scribblings, though it is not likely that the trained graphologist would rely wholly on them (if a sample of handwriting is not also available).

It is not possible to show every kind of doodle here; but these will serve as a basis for studying scribbles and trying to find their hidden meanings.

1. Formations which are made in a clearly patterned manner, boxes within boxes, etc., are signs of a mind that is well organized. This person usually plans well, and oversees his work in an efficient manner.

2. The doodles which have no definite form, and are just a mass (or a mess) of scribbled lines, may indicate a mind that is not relaxed, and it may be difficult for this person to think in a clear and concentrated manner. There may be tension about trifling matters.

3. The little stars show the person is an optimist, is able to meet disappointments without becoming discouraged about them.

4. The person who can think in a logical manner may scribble continuous formations in a rhythmic motion.

5. When games (such as tic-tac-toe) are used as the theme of the doodles, they show a competitive personality, a desire to win.

6. Decorated birds and animals are often scribbled by people who are highly imaginative, who may have a desire to write fiction.

7. The pretty face in a doodle reveals the person likes to be socially active, and that he enjoys meeting people in his work. This doodler likes people, and that's why he makes pretty faces.

8. But if he starts to draw ugly and distorted faces, he may be in a grouchy mood and doesn't like people, or he may not be too trusting a soul and may approach each person with skepticism.

9. Graceful wavy lines which follow a rhythmic pattern show a feeling for dancing and a musical appreciation.

1.
2.
3.
4
5.
6.
7.
8.
9.
10.
11.
12.
13.
14.
15.
LUV
LUV
16.

10. These of course are musical signs, and they reveal a good response to music.

11. The simple circles are a sign of spiritual aspirations, and optimism which is based on faith.

12. The little house shows a love for a peaceful home life. This may be drawn by the confirmed bachelor or spinster, or the very sophisticated person who scoffs at quiet home life. But the wee house betrays the innermost craving for domesticity, even though the outer manner seeks to impress others differently.

13. Arrows, ladders, or any other formations which aim at a target or at a high place reveal the person to be ambitious and anxious to shoot at a goal, or climb a ladder to get to the top.

14. Flowers and leaves and potted plants, when shown in doodles, are signs of a tender person who wants to be of direct service to others, to protect those in need.

15. What can be more indicative of a sentimentalist than little valentine hearts? A person with an outward gruff manner may make these doodles, if inwardly he is endowed with an affectionate heart.

16. The little doll is drawn by the one who has a strong maternal or paternal sense, who has a genuine fondness for youngsters.

The graphologist may be too subjective when attempting to analyze doodles, yet there may be some interesting results gleaned from them, especially when they are studied in conjunction with the handwriting.

IF NO DOODLES ARE MADE

Not everyone doodles. Those people who never doodle may have no conflict between their subconscious and conscious. However, this may not always be the case, so the handwriting analyst needs to be circumspect in making any definite statements in this direction. At all events, doodles are amusing, and they add a bit of spice to the process of analyzing personality through the handwriting formations.